Tons of Mone

Will Evans and Valentine

Adapted by
Alan Ayckbourn

Samuel French – London
New York – Sydney – Toronto – Hollywood

TONS OF MONEY

First presented in Alan Ayckbourn's revised version at the National Theatre, London on the 6th November, 1986, with the following cast of characters:

Sprules, a butler	Michael Gambon
Simpson, a parlourmaid	Diane Bull
Miss Benita Mullett	Barbara Hicks
Louise Allington	Polly Adams
Aubrey Henry Maitland Allington	Simon Cadell
Giles, a gardener	James Hayes
James Chesterman, a solicitor	Russell Dixon
Jean Everard	Marcia Warren
Henery	John Arthur
George Maitland	Michael Simkins

Directed by Alan Ayckbourn
Designed by Alan Tagg

The action of the play takes place in the library of Aubrey Henry Maitland Allington's house at Marlow

ACT I   Morning
ACT II   Three weeks later. Afternoon
ACT III The next day. Late afternoon

Time — 1922

The cover illustration is by Clive Francis and was originally used for the National Theatre's production and is here reproduced by kind permission of Clive Francis and the National Theatre

Please note that the original, earlier, version of Tons of Money is still available from Samuel French Ltd

ACT I

The library of Aubrey Henry Maitland Allington's house at Marlow. Morning

The room is handsomely furnished. At one side—double french windows, approached from the room by shallow steps, open to a terrace, commanding a view of the river and the landscape beyond. At the one side of the room is a low-backed armchair, and behind it, against the wall, a bronze statuette with an electrolier. A large settle couch with cushions is set at an angle, and at one end of it, a small square table on which is a telephone. In the wall of the window recess, facing the bookcase, is a low cabinet, and in the wall above it a speaking-tube. In the wall facing the audience, stands a grandfather clock

There are also large double doors which lead to a hall from which a stairway rises, and at the foot of the stairway a large leaded window. Also in the room a square, stone fireplace with irons in the hearth and a fender stool against the high curb. A gate-legged table, which at the rise of the curtain is laid for breakfast: two chairs are set at it. A winged armchair immediately below the fireplace and a smaller one facing it. The room has a high panelling, and the plain walls above this are decorated with tapestries

As the CURTAIN *rises the telephone bell rings; after a slight pause it rings again*

Sprules enters through the double doors; he is dressed in butler's morning clothes, is severe and precise in his manner, is slightly grey and wears side-whiskers. He carries a silver salver on which is the morning post. He puts this down as he takes up the telephone

Sprules Hello! Hello! . . . Yes, this is Mr Allington's house. . . . No, sir, the master isn't down yet. . . . I expect him any hour now, sir. . . . What name please, sir? . . . Mr Chest—Mr Chester—Mr Chesterman. . . . Very good, sir. I'll tell him you rang up. (*He replaces the receiver and picks up letters, writs, etc.*)

Simpson enters through the double doors carrying a tray with hot dishes, coffee and milk, which she places on the sideboard. She is a smart parlourmaid

Simpson Anything excitin', Mr Sprules?
Sprules Nothing much! (*He indicates that she should continue her duties. Studying the letters*) Hello, here we are again. Bill! Bill! Bill! (*He smells one*) Lady! And more bills!
Simpson Who's got most?
Sprules About fifty-fifty.

During the next Simpson lays out the breakfast

Simpson I never saw such a 'ouse.

Sprules And you never will again.

Simpson Do they ever pay anybody?

Sprules Not if they can help it.

Simpson I wonder the blooming creditors waste paper and ink sending the bills in.

Sprules Creditors, Miss Simpson, are like fishermen and lovers, they exist on hopes.

Miss Benita Mullett enters from the garden. She is an elderly lady, very brusque in manner and always speaks abruptly

Miss Mullett Simpson, have you seen my knitting?

Simpson (*finishing laying the table*) No, ma'am.

Miss Mullett One can't keep anything in this house. (*Seeing the breakfast table*) What! Breakfast not over yet!

Simpson (*on her way out*) Master and mistress just coming down, ma'am.

Miss Mullett What!

Sprules (*loudly*) Master and mistress are just coming down, ma'am.

Miss Mullett All right, don't shout, I'm not deaf. (*She takes the morning paper*) I never saw such a house! When I was a girl we always had breakfast at eight o'clock.

Louise Allington enters through the double doors. She is a young and pretty woman, very smartly dressed

Simpson steps aside to allow her to enter and then exits, closing the double doors

Louise Good-morning, Auntie Ben!

Miss Mullett (*severely*) Good-afternoon, my dear. (*She gives her cheek to be kissed*)

Louise kisses her cheek

D'you know it's eleven o'clock?

Louise Well, dear, what of it? (*She sits at the table and begins to look at her letters*)

Sprules, who has remained at the top of table, takes the covers off dishes

Miss Mullett Where's your husband?

Louise (*reading a letter*) Aubrey will be down soon—he's in his bath.

Miss Mullett The hours you and Aubrey keep, my dear, are a perfect disgrace.

Louise I loathe early rising.

Miss Mullett The early bird catches the worm, my dear.

Louise Well, if there's only one worm, Auntie, why should I spoil the market. (*She pours out coffee*)

Miss Mullett Your husband is worse than you are!

Louise Aubrey has the artistic temperament.

Miss Mullett What on earth does that mean?

Sprules has reached the double doors and prepares to leave

At that moment they burst open and Aubrey Henry Maitland Allington enters

Sprules recoils. Aubrey is a tall clean-shaven man of about thirty-five. He wears a smart lounge suit and monocle, and has a careless off-hand manner

Aubrey That's wonderful! Those bath salts have gone straight to my head. (*He goes up to the window, and inhales the air*)

Sprules exits through the double doors leaving them open

Good-morning, all! Good-morning, trees. Morning, birds. (*Noticing Miss Mullett*) Good-morning, Auntie Ben . . . (*He moves to her and, making a kissing noise with his lips, places his finger on her cheek. He moves to the table*)

During the next Miss Mullett wanders into the garden, momentarily, studying the newspaper

Good-morning, fish; good-afternoon, rolls. (*Picking up bills*) Good-night, bills. (*He sits at the breakfast table*)

Louise (*reading*) Here's a letter from my old friend Jean, Aubrey. She wants to come and stay some time.

Aubrey I've got bad news too.

Louise I haven't seen her for years and years.

Aubrey Yes, well, don't let's spoil it. (*He serves fish for Louise and himself*)

Louise (*reading another letter*) You know, Aubrey, I'm fed up with this dressmaker of mine.

Aubrey Wants money?

Louise Yes.

Aubrey I'll send her a cheque.

Louise Don't be silly, dear, it wouldn't be met.

Aubrey I beg your pardon, the day the bank refuses to meet my cheques, I shall take my overdraft elsewhere.

Miss Mullett (*returning from the garden, still reading*) An extensive V-shaped depression is rapidly approaching from the North Sea.

Aubrey That's her best friend Jean.

Miss Mullett (*reading*) Stormy weather may be expected. (*She puts down the newspaper*) Louise, you had better see about my galoshes.

During this Aubrey takes a writ out of an envelope. Miss Mullett moves into the garden but remains in view

Louise Yes, Auntie, I will. (*To Aubrey*) What's that funny paper you've got there?

Aubrey It's a writ.

Louise Really, what for?

Aubrey For those cigars I bought me to celebrate your last birthday.

Louise Well, Aubrey, you really mustn't be so generous in future.

Aubrey Sorry, darling, it's in the blood.

Miss Mullett (*from the garden*) Did you hear me, Louise? I said you'd better see about my galoshes.

Miss Mullett moves out of sight

Louise (*loudly*) Yes, Auntie, yes, yes! (*Softly*) Why doesn't she listen? If only she'd listen . . .
Miss Mullett (*now out of sight*) What's that?
Louise (*calling*) Nothing, Auntie. (*To herself*) Oh, dear.
Aubrey (*reading from another letter*) Now what the Dickens does this mean?
Louise Does what mean?
Aubrey (*reading*) Chesterman, Chesterman and Chesterman, Lincoln's Inn Fields . . .

Sprules enters from the double doors

Sprules Oh, I forgot to tell you, sir, a Mr Chesterman rang up this morning.
Aubrey I think he's written, too. Any message?
Sprules He asked if you were down, sir, and I said you weren't up.
Aubrey (*laughing*) You mean he asked if I was up, and you said I wasn't down. That's very good!
Sprules Er—yes, sir.
Aubrey All right, Sprules.
Sprules Very good, sir.

Sprules exits through the double doors, closing them

Aubrey (*reading*) Chesterman, Chesterman and Chesterman, Lincoln's Inn Fields.
Louise Why do West End solicitors always have three names in the firms?
Aubrey All the most dangerous things go in threes. Three-star brandy. Three-card trick. Three brass balls . . .
Louise What does it say?
Aubrey (*reading*) "Dear sir . . ."—he calls me dear—"Our Mr James Chesterman will call on you tomorrow morning at eleven o'clock to acquaint you with a matter of considerable importance to yourself. Faithfully yours, Chesterman, Chesterman (*turning over the letter*) and Chesterman." (*Thoughtfully*) Now is that a threat or a promise?
Louise He's either got some money to give us, or else wants some of ours.

Miss Mullett returns from the garden at this point. She moves across the room to the double doors during the next

Aubrey Darling, he's a solicitor.
Miss Mullett Who's a solicitor?
Louise Mr Chesterman, Auntie.
Miss Mullett Who's Mr Chesterman?
Aubrey The fellow we're talking about.
Miss Mullett Why?
Aubrey (*loudly and impatiently*) He's coming here.
Miss Mullett Don't shout, I'm not deaf. When's he coming?
Aubrey Any moment.

Miss Mullett What?

Aubrey }
Louise } (*together*) Any moment!

Miss Mullett Then I'm going. (*Opening the double doors*) My father used to say lawyers were like leeches. Only leeches do let you go sometimes.

Miss Mullett exits

Aubrey (*resuming breakfast*) I love having Auntie Ben here, she worries me to death.

Louise Poor dear Auntie, she means well.

Aubrey (*reading a letter*) Does she? Then, of course, there's no hope for her.

Louise By the way, dear, Fred Drury——

Aubrey February?

Louise No, Fred Drury!—called yesterday to see you. He wondered if you've forgotten you owe him a hundred pounds.

Aubrey Tell him I have forgotten it. Completely.

Louise I've a letter here from Robinson too, so——

Aubrey Robinson Crusoe?

Louise (*holding the letter*)—saying that if his account isn't paid by Friday, he'll commence proceedings.

Aubrey Well, I'm not stopping the man.

Louise (*irritably*) No; but Aubrey, do be serious. One can't run bills for ever.

Aubrey (*equally so*) One can try.

A slight pause

Louise What about your new invention?

Aubrey Which one, the hair restorer, the blasting powder, or the rat remover?

Louise The blasting powder.

Aubrey Oh! Gadinite? That's going to make our fortune.

Louise Fortune! How?

Aubrey Why, it's the most wonderful explosive that's ever been dreamt of. Now, say you're making a railway.

Louise I'm making a railway.

Aubrey No, darling. I mean imagine you're making a railway, you come to a mountain, what do you do?

Louise Look at it.

Aubrey No, damn it, blast it ... when you've done that the mountain's gone.

Louise Where's it gone to?

Aubrey Blown sky-high! (*Impressively*) D'you realize that one pinch of this powder, just as much as you could put on a ... sixpence, is enough to blow up the whole of half London—er—er—the half of whole London.

Louise (*awestruck*) Aubrey, are you going to sell your blasting powder in sixpenny packets?

Aubrey (*laughing*) It's going to make our fortune, that's all.

Louise Why, it'll be worth ... what will it be worth, Aubrey?

Aubrey One million and four pounds.
Louise Aubrey, but surely you can't be certain of the four.
Aubrey It's the four I'm certain of.

Giles appears at the french windows. He's a typical old gardener. He is carrying his hat, in which are three eggs. He comes into the room. Under the next he goes to the settle and very slowly takes the eggs one by one and places them on a cushion

Louise (*after a pause*) Then why not give a dinner-party to all the people we owe money to?
Aubrey We'd have to take the Albert Hall.
Louise And tell them about your new invention. It might keep them quiet. They'll have lots in common.
Aubrey You don't seem to realize that the people we've got to invite are the people we've got to . . . got to . . . go to . . . to go to . . . (*He trails off as they both see Giles*)
Louise Well, Giles?
Giles (*taking his time to answer*) Eggs!

He ambles slowly out of the french windows and exits

Aubrey and Louise both watch him intently until he disappears

Aubrey Little chatterbox! Why does he lay eggs in here—er—bring eggs in here?
Louise Poor old soul, he's proposed to Cook and she's refused him, so he won't go near the kitchen. (*Looking round the room*) Of course it's the expense of this big place that's doing all the mischief.
Aubrey Don't be silly, darling, there's only one way to get credit, that is make people believe you've got miles more money than you have.
Louise They can easily do that with us; look at this room for instance, anyone coming in here——
Aubrey Well, what's wrong with it? (*Taking up a letter*) That coat-of-arms isn't right, I admit, (*indicating the one over the fireplace*) it ought to be a couple of bailiffs rampant. (*Reading the letter*) Oh, Lord, that's done it . . .
Louise Done what?
Aubrey That account of Mannerings, they got judgement against us you know; this letter says that unless that five hundred pounds is paid within a week I'm bankrupt.

Louise groans in dismay

Don't worry, darling, you have to laugh. Well, you don't have to. But it's advisable.
Louise It's not much use giving that dinner then.

A gloomy pause. Louise is tearful

Sprules enters through the double doors

Sprules Mr Chesterman, sir.
Aubrey (*rising*) More trouble.

James Chesterman enters through the double doors. He is a clean-shaven man, very precise in manner, neatly dressed and carries an attaché case

Sprules exits through the double doors

Chesterman Mr Allington?

Aubrey rises, his plate of fish still in his hand

Aubrey Ah there you are, Mr Chesterman. (*He shakes hands*)
Louise (*rising*) I'd better go, Aubrey.
Aubrey No, no, no. Stay, dear. Mr Chesterman, my wife, my fish. Will you have some breakfast?
Chesterman No, thank you, I always breakfast at eight.
Aubrey We always dine at eight. Please sit down. (*Indicating the settle*) Oh, excuse me. (*He takes the eggs with the cushion and places them on another chair by table*) The gardener laid these—er—put them there.
Chesterman (*sitting*) I wrote to you last night, Mr Allington. My name is Chesterman, of the firm of Chesterman, Chesterman and Chesterman of Lincoln's Inn Fields.
Aubrey (*sitting*) Yes. I've just this moment opened your letter.
Chesterman You'll permit me to ask you a few questions?
Aubrey Certainly, certainly and certainly.
Chesterman I'm right, I think, in believing that you are Aubrey Henry Maitland Allington?
Aubrey Yes, all of them.
Chesterman Son of the late Charles Rodney Maitland Allington of Wintercroft in the county of Devon?
Aubrey I've always understood so.
Chesterman You have a brother, John Basil Whittingham Allington, sometime resident of Baffin Bay?
Aubrey (*tersely*) Yes, but that's not my fault.
Chesterman Please answer my question, Mr Allington. Is that so?
Aubrey I regret to say it is.
Chesterman That is an expression I can neither endorse nor contradict.
Aubrey You never knew my brother.
Chesterman I didn't.
Aubrey Obviously.
Chesterman Mr Allington, your brother I believe once did you some injury.
Aubrey You're right. (*Rising*) It was some injury. He married the only girl I ever loved!
Louise Aubrey!
Aubrey Oh, before I met you.
Louise Yes, but you never told me.
Aubrey I was too broke—broken-hearted. My brother's last action—Mr Chesterman, my brother's last action——
Chesterman Mr Allington, your brother's last action was to—die a week ago.
Aubrey I'm sorry!
Chesterman Your brother has left you——

Aubrey (*scornfully*) His kind wishes?

Chesterman A life interest in his entire fortune.

Louise (*standing, in surprise*) A life interest in his entire fortune?

Chesterman Yes, madam—expressing at the same time his sincere regrets for any injury he might have done you.

Louise (*thoughtfully, after a pause*) I wonder if it's too late to send the dear fellow a nice wreath?

Aubrey (*to Louise*) Allow me, dear, the head of the house. Mr Chesterman, what can I say?

Louise (*reprovingly*) Nothing, dear.

Aubrey Nothing, dear.

Chesterman The estate—I am quoting from figures sent me from Alaska——

Aubrey Bless you!

Chesterman —amounts roughly to four hundred and seventy thousand dollars.

Aubrey (*excitedly walking up and down*) Four—hundred and seventy thousand—dollars!!!

Chesterman Yes.

Aubrey gazes at him for a moment and then begins to laugh, Louise joining in

Aubrey I'll buy it.

Chesterman (*puzzled*) You'll buy what, Mr Allington?

Aubrey Yes—I mean, what am I expected to say?

Chesterman I'm afraid I don't understand you.

Aubrey Well, what's the joke?

Chesterman Mr Allington, I don't know what you're driving at. If you are casting aspersions on my—— (*He rises*)

Aubrey No, no, no! I beg your pardon! But is it really true?

Chesterman Here is the will. (*He takes a will from his briefcase*)

Aubrey takes the will from Chesterman; Louise in turn takes it from Aubrey

Aubrey And it amounts to what, you say?

Chesterman As far as can be at present ascertained, four hundred and seventy thousand dollars.

Louise I think he might have left it in pounds. (*She studies the will*)

Chesterman In Alaska they speak of everything in dollars, madam.

Louise Are there sixteen dollars to the pound, Aubrey, same as ounces?

Aubrey It depends on the height of the sea-level, darling.

Chesterman Your interest, Mr Allington, is only a life one.

Aubrey That won't worry me.

Chesterman In the event of your death, the money passes to your cousin, George Maitland of Mexico.

Aubrey He'll never get it.

Chesterman And why not, pray?

Aubrey He's gone to a place where they don't issue return tickets.

Chesterman I beg your pardon.

Aubrey Cousin George had a sticky end in a whisky saloon in Mexico.

Chesterman So I've heard, Mr Allington, but no-one seems to know positively what actually occurred.

Aubrey The only other party who could tell us, Mr Chesterman, was so full of George's bullets that he had no further interest in the proceedings.

Chesterman All the same we have no actual proof of death.

Aubrey No, George had the proof.

Chesterman All the same, we are advertising for him.

Aubrey Well, unless they issue asbestos editions I don't think it will reach him.

Chesterman Still, dead or alive, let's hope he won't be wanted for a long time.

Aubrey I entirely agree.

Chesterman And now I must leave you, merely congratulating you on your good fortune, and hoping you will both live long to enjoy it.

Aubrey (*shaking hands*) Spoken like a true friend and a Special Constable.

Chesterman (*crossing to Louise*) Goodbye, Mrs Allington. (*He shakes hands*) I will leave you that copy of the will. If there is any immediate advance——

Aubrey What's that?

Louise Immediate advance, dear.

Chesterman goes towards the double doors

Aubrey (*excitedly—crossing to Chesterman*) Oh, yes, yes, certainly, make it as immediate as possible. Goodbye, Mr Chesterman, goodbye. It can't be too immediate.

Chesterman exits through the double doors

Aubrey, standing at the double doors, shouts after him

Goodbye, Mr Chesterman! Take any hat you like!

Aubrey and Louise stand facing one another

Louise Aubrey, I think I want to scream or dance!

Aubrey Well, darling, scream and dance, we can afford it, now!

Both rush to one another, embrace, laughing loudly and excitedly

Sprules enters through the double doors; he stands amazed

They both stop guiltily

Sprules Did you call, sir?

Aubrey No, no, Sprules, we were merely screaming, that's all.

Sprules Very good, sir.

Sprules, looking puzzled, exits closing the doors

Louise and Aubrey resume their former excitement. Aubrey throws cushions about, takes a pile of letters, bills, etc. from the table

Aubrey Look, darling. (*He throws bills in the air*) There they go, full pack.

Louise, who is still clutching the will tosses it in the air for good measure

Louise (*falling into a chair*) I feel better now.

Aubrey (*about to sit on the eggs*) So do I. (*Rising before he does so*) Now where's that will? (*Not seeing it at first, perturbed*) Darling, it was here a minute ago. I haven't thrown it away, have I?

Louise (*helping him to find it, picking a writ up from the floor*) Here it is, darling.

Aubrey (*taking it from her, and throwing it back on the floor*) No, darling, that's a writ. (*Finding it*) Ah, there's the will. Now, let's have a look at it. (*He becomes very important*) Don't get excited, darling; have you never had money left you before? I have, all mine's left me. (*Reading*) "I, John Basil Whittingham Allington, being of sound mind——"

Louise What dear?

Aubrey Being of sound mind, dear. They have to put that in to account for his going to a solicitor.

Louise I see.

Aubrey "I give, bequeath and devise all my real and personal estate of which I may die possessed or to whom I may hereinafter become entitled together with all lands, estates, here—here—dit . . ."

Louise Here-dit-a-ments.

Aubrey "Here-dit-a-ments, tenements, massages . . ."

Louise Messuages.

Aubrey "Sewages or any other properties."

Louise I see now why they put that bit in about the sound mind.

Aubrey Never mind, we don't want to understand it. We'll take a month's holiday and study it. (*He folds it up and places it in the toast rack*) Four hundred and seventy thousand dollars.

Louise Four hundred and seventy thousand dollars.

Aubrey That's about one hundred and twenty thousand pounds, about six thousand a year. Why, it's a fortune! (*He picks up the receiver of the telephone*) Am I there? Yes. (*He replaces the receiver*)

Louise There's simply nothing we can't afford.

Aubrey One hundred and twenty thousand pounds! We can pay off every bill we owe.

Louise What's that?

Aubrey I say we can pay off every bill we owe.

Louise Yes, but——

Aubrey But what, we've got tons of money.

Louise (*deliberately*) But we owe tons of money, Aubrey, and by the time we've paid for the tons of money, there won't be any tons of money left.

Aubrey And we'll be bankrupt next week.

Louise It will all be taken by the official retriever.

Aubrey Oh, Lord, I'd forgotten that.

Louise But our creditors won't.

Aubrey They'll simply swarm round us now.

Louise Of course they will.

Aubrey Like a flock of wasps.

Louise Do wasps flock, Aubrey?

Aubrey Yes, if they want to.

Louise Oh, I never knew they did.

Aubrey Whom do we owe money to?

Louise Everyone we've ever dealt with.

Aubrey Shall I make a list? (*Picking up an envelope from the floor*)

Louise Of the people we owe money to?

Aubrey No, of the people we don't—it would be miles quicker.

Louise Aubrey, don't fool. It's too serious.

Aubrey It's perfectly disgusting, you know, the way people give credit.

Louise I think they ought to make it a criminal offence.

Aubrey They simply don't deserve to be paid!

Louise Besides, think how hurt your brother would be if he thought we'd used his money to give to people he didn't even know.

Aubrey Well, what are we to do?

Louise Is it necessary for our creditors to know we've come into money?

Aubrey My dear girl, how can we prevent it? They're bound to know.

Louise Yes, I suppose so.

Aubrey Of course they'd know if I had five shillings. They'd know like a shot.

Pause

Louise (*suddenly*) Aubrey, I've got an idea!

Aubrey What?

Louise What happens if you die?

Aubrey I shall probably be buried.

Louise Don't be absurd! I mean, who gets the money?

Aubrey George Maitland, my first cousin. Chesterman just told us so!

Louise But you say he's dead.

Aubrey So he is.

Louise Sure?

Aubrey Absolutely. Positive!

Louise Then why not—bring him—to life again.

Aubrey D'you think I'm a corpse reviver?

Louise You're very dense, dear! If once we can kill you——

Aubrey Eh?

Louise If once we can make people believe you're dead, you can come to life again as George Maitland, your cousin, and claim all the money.

Aubrey contemplates her slowly as her meaning dawns on him

Aubrey By Jove, what a brain wave.

Louise That's what I thought.

Aubrey You mean——? Let's figure this out!

Louise You've got to die! And there must be no mistake about it.

Aubrey But how am I going to die?

Louise Never mind that now. You're dead!

Aubrey Yes.

Louise Your will is read. You leave everything to me!

Aubrey But, darling, there's nothing to leave.

Louise Exactly, that's what I'm driving at!

Aubrey What's the good if there's——Oh, I see! And so the poor dog had none. (*He points to the bills on the table*) The Retriever!

Louise Quite so. Exit crowd of sorrowing creditors.

Aubrey (*laughing*) Can't you see them all coming to the funeral with eyes full of writs and pockets full of tears? Well, I'm dead—now what happens?

Louise Now George Maitland appears.

Aubrey I see—that's me.

Louise Exactly—what's George like?

Aubrey crosses to the sideboard and produces a photo album

Aubrey (*as he does so*) I've got a photo he sent after he'd been out in Mexico a few years. (*He turns over several pages until he locates the picture*) There.

Louise (*studying the album*) Oh, is that George? How tall is he?

Aubrey Oh, he's a fine-looking, big strapping chap—just about my build. (*Bracing himself as he says this*)

Louise Could you make yourself look like that, Aubrey?

Aubrey Oh, easily.

Louise But he's quite good looking.

Aubrey Exactly.

Louise Then that's settled. Chesterman has advertised for you, I mean for George.

Aubrey (*striving to follow her*) George . . .

Louise Well then, after you're dead, wait a few weeks, and then send a wire to Chesterman . . .

Aubrey Chesterman . . .

Louise "Just landed in England. Seen your advertisement."

Aubrey Advertisement . . .

Louise "I am on my way down. George Maitland."

Aubrey Down . . . Shall I be able to stay here?

Louise Of course! We're cousins!

Aubrey And after everything's fixed up, we can get married.

Louise How ripping! Fancy, having a second honeymoon with one's own husband.

The double doors have opened a fraction. Sprules is peering through the gap

Aubrey It's never done, darling, but we'll try it. Now, the next thing is—— (*He becomes aware that they are not alone*) What do you want, Sprules?

Sprules Miss Mullett wants to know if she left her wool here, sir?

Aubrey Tell Miss Mullett to go to the—the dining-room. It isn't here.

Sprules Very good, sir.

Sprules exits, closing the double doors

Louise Well . . .

Aubrey silences her and opens the double doors swiftly. Sprules has gone. He closes them and motions for her to continue

How are you going to die?

Aubrey I don't know, I've never done it before.
Louise We've got to bury you too.
Aubrey Well, don't harp on it.
Louise We mustn't forget to put it in all the papers.
Aubrey Have you made a hobby of this sort of thing?
Louise No, dear, but it's most essential that there shouldn't be any doubt whatsoever regarding your death.
Aubrey (*grimly*) There won't be any by the time you've finished with me.
Louise What's worrying me is how you're going to die. We must get the details right.
Aubrey Well, don't get them too right.

A slight pause, during which both think deeply

Louise What about a nice fit?
Aubrey No, thanks, the moment I start throwing fits, Sprules will come in and sit on my head.
Louise I thought it was rather a good idea.
Aubrey I'm sorry to differ from you, dear; I think it's a pretty bad idea. People get over fits.
Louise I'd take good care you didn't.

Aubrey looks at Louise suspiciously

Aubrey (*deliberately*) Well, anyhow—fits—are—off!

Another pause. Louise acts out one or two other ideas, silently. Aubrey watches her apprehensively

Louise (*thoughtfully*) You wouldn't like to hang yourself from the banisters, dear?
Aubrey No, I shouldn't.
Louise Or throw yourself slightly out of the window?
Aubrey Certainly not. You can't throw yourself slightly out of a window, you either do it all or none at all.
Louise I thought you might.
Aubrey Well, think again.
Louise Aubrey, if you could only cut your throat.
Aubrey What!
Louise (*hastily*) Oh, not much, darling, only a teeny little bit.
Aubrey Oh, I thought you meant cut it right off.
Louise It would be the making of us, Aubrey!
Aubrey (*irritably*) You've got a mind like a Newgate Calendar.
Louise (*crossly*) Well, you can't turn up as George Maitland until you are dead, so you may as well decide quickly how you are going to die.

Giles enters with flowers from the french windows

Aubrey No! If I'm going to die, what I really want is——
Giles Flowers. (*He places the flowers beside Aubrey*)

Giles exits through the french windows

Aubrey (*edging away from the flowers*) I've taken a sudden dislike to flowers. How can I be killed at once?

Sprules opens the double doors, speaks from there

Sprules Any orders for the butcher?
Aubrey (*starting*) No! Run away— we're busy.
Louise I'll see you later, Sprules.

Sprules exits, closing the double doors

Aubrey I never saw such a house. One can't even arrange to die quietly.
Louise We must find a way.
Aubrey Well, darling, I've thought over here, and I've thought over there ...

A slight pause

Louise Aubrey! We could explode you!
Aubrey What?
Louise That's the idea! The blasting powder.
Aubrey Explode me!!
Louise Yes, we'll have a nice explosion and you can be blown to bits.
Aubrey Oh! Let me tell you, madam, we are not going to be exploded. I'm sorry—any other time I can do anything to oblige you——
Louise Listen! I want you to go down into your workshop at the bottom of the garden and make a heap of all the most explosive things you've got on one of the tables.
Aubrey (*sarcastically*) Then sit on it, and light a pipe.
Louise You know that speaking-tube in the workshop—the other end of that? (*She indicates the speaking-tube*)
Aubrey Yes—well?
Louise Draw the table close up to it and put a lighted candle on it so that it stands touching the end of the speaking-tube.
Aubrey Well?
Louise Round the candle you can pile gunpowder with a trail leading to all the new blasting powder.
Aubrey Yes?
Louise The moment I blow down the tube it will knock the candle over, which will fire the gunpowder, which will burn the trail which will light the blasting powder which will cause a terrible explosion which will blow the whole place sky-high. There you are!
Aubrey Pardon me! There I'm not.
Louise Of course you're not, you're miles away by then. You've told the servants you're not to be disturbed ...
Aubrey Yes?
Louise But five minutes before the explosion you've locked the door, and got away unnoticed.
Aubrey Oh, and they still think I'm there.
Louise Exactly. At twelve o'clock—I'll come in and say "Where's the master?"

Aubrey And they'll say: "He's in his workshop, ma'am, and isn't to be disturbed till twelve o'clock."

Louise That's it. Then at twelve o'clock I'll blow down the tube and they'll spend the rest of the day hunting for pieces of you . . .

Aubrey Ripping!

Louise In the meantime, you will have crept up to the attic, packed a bag with all the things you will require for about three weeks, and take all the loose cash you can find about——

Aubrey I've done that.

Louise Then you can get away when the coast is clear.

Aubrey Ripping! When shall I turn up as Cousin George?

Louise Give it three weeks, it will look better.

Aubrey Yes, but in any case I'll ring up before I arrive. (*He kisses her*) Ha, ha! I'm glad I thought of that idea!

Louise Of course. Now I'll ring for Sprules. (*She goes and rings the bell*) Remember I shan't blow down the speaking-tube till twelve o'clock.

Aubrey Funny to think that when next we meet, I shall be dead.

Louise Darling! It will be the wisest thing you've ever done. Goodbye, darling. (*She kisses him*) See you in three weeks.

Sprules enters through the double doors

Yes, clear away, Sprules.

Louise exits through the double doors

Aubrey starts singing nervously—he catches sight of Sprules

Aubrey Oh, Sprules—what's the matter, man?

Sprules You're looking a little pale, sir.

Aubrey I'm feeling a little pale. I've got a wonderful idea, Sprules.

Sprules Yes, sir?

Simpson enters with a tray through the double doors and starts to clear the breakfast things from the table

Sprules starts picking up the strewn letters etc.

Aubrey And I'm going down to my workshop to experiment.

Sprules Yes, sir.

Aubrey I mustn't on any account be disturbed, Sprules.

Sprules I'll see that you're not, sir.

Aubrey You see, I'm working on some very high explosives, Sprules.

Sprules Yes, sir.

Aubrey Frightfully high explosives, Sprules. So high that if they exploded you'd never find a bit of me again.

Sprules Very good, sir.

Aubrey In fact, Sprules, they're so high that I'd rather nobody left the house till I've finished.

Sprules Yes, sir.

Aubrey That will be, say—approximately (*he looks at his watch*) say twelve o'clock precisely, Sprules.

Sprules Yes, sir.
Aubrey And if I am killed, don't bother to lay me out for lunch, Sprules . . .
lay out . . . lunch for me . . .
Sprules No, sir.

Miss Mullett enters through the double doors

Miss Mullett Oh, I was looking for you, Aubrey.
Aubrey I'm just going down to my workshop, Auntie.
Miss Mullett I'll come with you. (*She moves after him*)
Aubrey (*quickly*) Oh, no, no, no!
Miss Mullett And why not, pray?
Aubrey You can come—er—after twelve o'clock precisely. Not a moment
before. I've got some frightfully dangerous work on and I wouldn't have
anyone near me.
Miss Mullett Very well, have it your own way. (*She sits down and begins
knitting*)
Aubrey And, Sprules, if any of my creditors call, tell them to come round
again—after twelve! After twelve, Sprules, don't forget. Precisely.
Sprules Precisely, sir.

*Simpson has cleared the breakfast things, removing the will from the toast
rack and leaving it on the table. She exits through the double doors*

Aubrey exits into the garden through the french windows

*Sprules goes to clear the tablecloth. He sees the will, and taking care he is not
observed, examines the document, reacts and furtively slips it into his pocket*

Miss Mullett Where's Giles, Sprules?
Sprules (*guiltily*) I don't know, ma'am; shall I find him for you?
Miss Mullett What?
Sprules (*loudly*) I say, shall I find him for you?
Miss Mullett Don't shout, man! I'm not deaf!
Sprules Can I give him a message for you, ma'am?
Miss Mullett No, it doesn't matter; I told him to bring me a cucumber so
that I can make the salad for lunch. (*She looks at her watch*)

Simpson enters through the double doors with a telegram

Giles enters with a cucumber through the french windows

Yes, Simpson?
Simpson Telegram for the master, ma'am.

*Sprules exits through the french windows with the tablecloth from which he
intends to shake the crumbs*

Miss Mullett Well, give it to me. He's in his workshop and doesn't want to
be disturbed. I'll call and tell him.

Simpson comes to her and gives her the telegram

Giles (*on the steps of the window*) Cucumber!

Miss Mullett Oh, there you are, Giles—you're late.

Simpson exits through the double doors

Giles (*looking at the grandfather clock*) I ain't late—you said twelve o'clock—ain't twelve o'clock.

Miss Mullett It is twelve o'clock. That clock's slow.

Giles You needn't shout, 'm—I ain't deaf! (*He puts the clock on to twelve o'clock*)

Miss Mullett (*speaking under her breath*) Oh, what impudence—impertinent——(*She goes to the speaking-tube, removes it from the wall and is about to blow down it when . . .*)

Louise enters through the double doors

(*Seeing her*) Oh, Louise, I'm just——

Louise (*alarmed*) Auntie! No! Stop!

Miss Mullett There's a telegram for Aubrey, my dear—I was going to tell him.

Louise (*grabbing the speaking-tube from Miss Mullett*) Well, you mustn't. Not yet.

Giles Please, 'm I——

Louise One minute, Giles . . . (*To Miss Mullett*) Aubrey mustn't be disturbed, Auntie, until——

Miss Mullett Until what, my dear?

Louise Until twelve o'clock, Auntie!

Miss Mullett It is twelve o'clock now, dear.

Louise What! (*She turns round and looks at the clock*) Why, so it is. (*She goes across to the speaking-tube*)

Giles Please 'm——(*Trying to get a word in*)

Louise Do be quiet a minute, Giles. (*She gives a violent blow down the speaking-tube and replaces it. To Giles*) Now, what is it, Giles?

Giles Oh, I only wanted to tell you, 'm, I just put that clock on ten minutes.

Louise What!!! (*She gazes at Giles in horror*)

A tremendous explosion is heard. Miss Mullett, Giles and Louise rush wildly to the french windows

Sprules runs in from the garden. His tablecloth is charred and smouldering

Simultaneously, Simpson rushes on from the double doors shouting and screaming

Debris from the explosion, bricks, tiles, fragments of plaster, etc., is falling. Sprules, waving his arms about wildly, ushers them back through the double doors, shouting:

Sprules Giles! Giles! Simpson! Save yourselves!

They all rush out through the double doors . . . leaving Louise in mental agony. Smoke is seen through the french windows. Louise sinks into an armchair. Silence

Louise I've killed him, I've killed him.

An approaching cry and Aubrey drops through the ceiling by the french windows. His face is blackened with gunpowder, his clothes are hanging on him in shreds. He gazes wildly around as he staggers to his feet. He points angrily at his pocket watch as —

the CURTAIN *falls*

ACT II

The same. Three weeks have elapsed. Afternoon

At the rise of the Curtain, *Louise is discovered lying on the settle; she is reading a novel, she is in deep mourning, but her attitude shows complete indifference, and she is laughing over her book. After a slight pause the telephone rings. The moment she hears it Louise puts her book aside and assumes the role of grief-stricken widow. She allows the telephone to ring*

In a moment or so, Sprules enters through the double doors. He tip-toes to the phone on the table and brings the instrument to Louise

Sprules The telephone, madam.
Louise (*taking the phone and answering wearily*) Hello! ... Yes, Mrs Allington speaking. ... Who? ... Mr George Maitland? ... Oh, good-afternoon, Mr Maitland.

Sprules reacts. He lingers at the double doors, hoping to hear the conversation. Louise looks at him

He exits

When the doors close, Louise's voice and expression change

Yes, yes, is that you, Aubrey darling? ... All right, I'll call you George. (*Laughing*) I must get used to it. Everything all right? ... You'll be down in half an hour, good! ... But it's deadly dull being a widow ... (*Laughing*) Oh, yes, all in black. ... Where are you now? ... Where? ... No, that's pronounced Reading, Aubrey. ... They couldn't bury you, Aubrey, because they couldn't find anything of you to bury. (*Laughing*) Oh, Aubrey, I mean George, I wish there was some way I could be sure of recognizing you when you come in. ... What? ... You'll be singing—oh, Aubrey, I never knew you had a voice. (*Laughing*) All right, dear, you shall have the room next to mine ...

Sprules has opened the double doors a fraction and stands listening

Louise, aware of this, changes her tone again

Then I'll expect you in half an hour, Mr Maitland. Goodbye. (*She hangs up the receiver*) We must prepare a room for Mr Maitland, Sprules
Sprules That'll be the spare room, ma'am?
Louise Er—no, Sprules. I think you'd better put him in the blue room.
Sprules (*surprised*) The one next to yours, ma'am?
Louise Yes, I think so. It's a more attractive room.
Sprules Very good, ma'am.

Simpson enters through the double doors, with tea things (for four) on the tray of the butler's table. She has a tea-cloth over her arm

Louise crosses to the windows

Louise Has Miss Everard arrived yet?
Simpson Not yet, ma'am.
Louise It's quite time she was here. I think I'll walk down and meet her.

Louise exits through the french windows

Sprules (*waiting till she has disappeared; to Simpson*) Now what does she want to put him in the room next to hers for? (*He sets up the legs of the butler's table*)
Simpson Who's "him"?
Sprules Mr Maitland.
Simpson Well, why shouldn't she?
Sprules (*mysteriously*) Who do you think is coming here this afternoon?
Simpson (*puzzled*) Mr George Maitland, you just said.
Sprules Mr George Maitland don't exist—he's dead.
Simpson Well, if 'e's dead, 'ow can 'e be coming 'ere today?
Sprules He isn't—but she thinks he is. (*He looks round to see they are not overheard*)
Simpson Wot on earth are you drivin' at, Mr Sprules?
Sprules Listen! The poor guv'nor being dead, the money goes to his cousin, George Maitland of Mexico.
Simpson 'Ow do you know?
Sprules 'Cos I've seen it in the will. I come across it in the drawer after the poor master's death, so I took the liberty of reading it.
Simpson Well?
Sprules Now, I happens to know too, that George Maitland of Mexico is dead, but they've never had actual proof of his death, so they've advertised for him. (*He looks round to make certain no-one is about*)
Simpson Yes?
Sprules Well, I says to myself: "Sprules," I says, "it's a lot of money it is, and you want to get married . . ."
Simpson (*coyly*) Oh, Mr Sprules.

He goes to take her hands romantically but she is twisting the tea-cloth excitedly

Sprules Don't fidget with that thing! (*He snatches the tea-cloth away and puts it aside*) "But George Maitland is dead, so he can never get it."
Simpson (*puzzled*) Go on.
Sprules But if someone exactly like him came along and said: "I'm George Maitland from Mexico, and I claim that money"—they'd have to brass up.
Simpson So you've got someone to dress up as George Maitland, and it's him who's coming here today.
Sprules You've got it.
Simpson Who is he?

Sprules My brother Henery.

Simpson What, him who's at Drury Lane; then that's why he came to see you yesterday.

Sprules That's right—I had to prime him up and show him the photo of the real George Maitland so that he could know what to make up like. If this comes off it means tons of money for us.

Simpson Then—we shall be able to get married, Mr Sprules. (*She is twisting the tea-towel in her hands again*)

Sprules (*moving to her to take her hands*) Yes ... (*He irritably snatches the towel from her again and throws it aside*) And we can clear away to a nice little country cottage, and no-one will be any the wiser. (*He kisses her*)

Simpson Have you fixed it all up?

Sprules I've put my brother through his paces. He got the wind up about it, but I told him it was as easy as falling off a log. (*Anxiously*) Henery should be able to bring it off. If he can keep himself in hand.

Simpson How ever do you mean?

Sprules (*confidentially*) He's a devil with the ladies. That's his problem. Uncontrollable. He can't resist them; they can't keep their hands off him.

Simpson (*coyly*) It runs in the family, then, Mr Sprules.

Sprules (*admonishing her, but not displeased*) Now, now, now. (*Resuming*) He was on the telephone to the mistress just a minute ago. I'd arranged for him to come tomorrow, but he must have changed his mind.

Simpson What's he like?

Sprules You can't mistake him, he's got a brown beard and moustache— he'll announce himself as George Maitland—and I've arranged that if we want to warn him to signal like this. Number one—(*business scratching elbow*) that means—be careful. Number two—(*business rubbing ear*) that means—danger, and number three—(*business rubbing nose and making a clicking noise with mouth*)—come into the kitchen.

Simpson imitates him

Don't make that noise.

Simpson You did it.

Sprules Yes, I know, but I am trying to explain things to you. And if we can't catch his eye, we've got to drop something so as to draw his attention. Like this ... (*He picks up a tray from a side table and drops it*)

Simpson If it's very important?

Sprules Yes, not otherwise.

He indicates for Simpson to pick up the tray. She does so

Simpson You have got a wonderful brain, Mr Sprules.

Sprules again goes to take her hands. Simpson drops her tea-cloth hastily

Sprules (*proudly*) A good butler is like a patent medicine—there's nothing he can't do.

They kiss

Giles enters along the terrace pushing an aged, squeaking wheelbarrow. He meets Louise and Jean Everard who is dressed in travelling costume. Louise leans on her arm, speaking very sadly and feebly

Simpson and Sprules hastily resume their duties

Simpson goes straight out through the double doors

Jean He keeps the garden beautifully.

Giles goes off the other way

Louise Yes, dear, but he's a terrible nuisance, he's always having trouble with Cook. (*To Sprules*) Sprules, go and see about Miss Everard's luggage.
Sprules Yes, ma'am.

Miss Mullett has entered through the double doors, one knitting needle in her hand, obviously in search of the rest of her knitting

Sprules exits past her and closes the doors behind him

Miss Mullett Ah, Louise, have you seen the rest of this . . . ? (*She waves the knitting needle*)
Louise Auntie, this is Miss Everard—my aunt, Miss Mullett.

Jean and Miss Mullett shake hands

Jean Everard is an old friend of mine, Auntie.
Jean I simply had to come down and see her, Miss Mullett. Poor Louise.
Miss Mullett Deplorable business . . . (*She continues her search*)

Louise takes out her handkerchief, sobbing

Jean (*turning to her*) There, there, darling, don't cry!
Louise Poor darling Aubrey!
Jean Such a sudden end, too!
Louise Yes, ten minutes before he expected it.
Jean What, darling?
Louise I said—so unexpected. (*She goes and sits*)
Jean (*to Miss Mullett softly*) I suppose—er—nothing was found of him?
Miss Mullett What!
Jean (*loudly*) I said, I suppose nothing was found of him.

Louise wails

Miss Mullett You needn't shout—I'm not deaf.
Louise (*tearfully*) They found a trouser button, but they weren't sure whether it was his or Sprules', apparently they both went to the same tailor.

Miss Mullett goes out through the french windows and searches in the garden

Jean My dear, I had rather a shock today. (*She sits near Louise*)
Louise Really, dear?
Jean Yes, just now, I thought I saw my husband.
Louise Jean, I never knew you were married.

Jean I know, I never told you. You see my husband is dead, too.

Louise Oh, my darling! But your name?

Jean Oh, yes, you see we were married secretly, we were just going to announce our marriage when he was called away to South America on urgent business. I never saw him again.

Louise Never saw him again?

Jean No, I heard later that he had been shot.

Louise Shot!

Jean (*proudly*) He gave his life for another.

Louise Oh! How heroic of him.

Jean (*sighing*) I knew he was a hero when he married me; from the day he met me he never looked at another girl.

Louise How wonderful!

Jean Of course, if one can really trust one's husband ...

Louise Oh, I know I trusted Aubrey implicitly, but not out of my sight. But today, darling, what happened today?

Jean Oh, yes, of course! I was sitting in my compartment when a man got in. I was reading my paper, and I shouldn't have looked up, only he started humming a tune that my husband used to love when we were first married—I can't remember the name of it, but it went like this. (*She sings to the tune of "Ta-ra-ra-boom-de-ay"*)

Louise I seem to have heard that tune somewhere. Oh yes, Aubrey and I used to love it, too ... (*She sings*) De–de–de–de–de–de. It's out of one of the Gilbert and Sullivan Operas, I think.

Miss Mullett whose search has taken her back near the french windows has heard this last

Miss Mullett Would you mind doing that again?

Jean and Louise sing together—Miss Mullett joining in

I know! It's out of one of the oratorios.

Jean I rather think it is, Miss Mullett. (*To Louise*) At any rate, it gave me quite a shock. Then suddenly he turned round—and, darling, it was my husband to the life.

Louise Darling—what did you do?

Jean I said "Darling"—just like that. And then I think I fainted.

Miss Mullett Why?

Louise The shock, Auntie, of course.

Miss Mullett What shock?

Louise (*aside*) Oh, dear, oh, dear! (*Aloud*) Miss Everard thought she——

Miss Mullett Don't shout, dear, it's all right.

Louise Miss Everard thought she saw her husband.

Miss Mullett Is she married?

Louise Yes.

Miss Mullett Is he enough to make her faint?

Louise No, no, no! But he's dead.

Miss Mullett (*finally*) Well, if he's dead, she couldn't have seen him.

Miss Mullett exits through the double doors

Louise gives a movement to indicate to Jean how hopeless it is to converse with her aunt

Louise Oh, dear. Darling, did you see him again?
Jean No; when I came to he'd completely disappeared.
Louise But didn't you ask the officials?
Jean Yes, but they hadn't seen anybody.
Louise How extraordinary!
Louise Jean, you don't think you could have been mistaken?
Jean Dear, I'd know my own husband anywhere.
Louise What's he like?
Jean Well, he's got a big bushy beard and he used to love it when I stroked it.

Sprules enters through the double doors

Sprules Mr Chesterman, ma'am.

Chesterman enters through the double doors. He is filled with appropriate solemnity at a widow's grief

Simpson enters behind him with a teapot which she places on the tea table

Louise (*rising*) How do you do, Mr Chesterman? (*She shakes hands with him*) Jean, this is Mr Chesterman—Miss Everard.

They bow

Sprules and Simpson exit through the double doors

Will you have some tea?

They sit. Louise pours tea for the three of them

Chesterman I've had a wire from your late husband's cousin, Mrs Allington, and he's coming down here to call on you.
Louise Yes, I'm expecting him here today.
Chesterman Really?
Louise (*passing a cup to Jean*) He rang me up to say he was coming down.
Jean I'm quite looking forward to seeing him.
Chesterman Of course you know, Mrs Allington, that owing to the sad death of your poor husband——
Louise Poor dear Aubrey!
Chesterman —you now become entitled to the whole of the money at the death of your late husband's cousin, the present heir.
Louise (*amazed*) I do?
Chesterman You do.
Louise (*holding out a cup for Chesterman*) But—you never told me.
Chesterman (*rising and crossing to take it from her*) I left you a copy of the will.
Louise Yes, but my husband couldn't understand it.
Chesterman I have often heard such remarks.
Louise I wish Aubrey had known that before.

Chesterman I beg your pardon.

Louise (*hurriedly*) I mean he would have—er—it would have comforted him to know that I was—er—provided for.

Jean It would have made a difference to him.

Louise Oh, it would have made a great difference to him!

A pause. Jean serves bread and butter to both Chesterman and herself. Louise refuses

Chesterman I'm sorry to say, Mrs Allington, that your husband's estate is working out worse than we thought.

Louise Poor dear fellow! He was always so generous to me.

Jean Was he, darling?

Louise Yes—he gave me everything credit could buy.

Jean (*consolingly*) Dear, you must try and be brave.

Louise Yes ...

Jean Remember you have a part to play now.

Louise I have ...

Jean He would want you to play it well!

Louise He said so!

Jean I speak as one widow to another. (*Sobbing*)

In the garden a man's voice is heard singing—"Ta-ra-ra-boom-de-ay." All rise. Louise walks briskly to the windows

Louise Who's this?

Jean Excuse me ... (*She moves to one corner of the room and repairs her make-up, not really noticing the ensuing scene*)

Aubrey appears from the garden. He is disguised as George Maitland, and wears a brown suit, has a beard and a moustache, rather tanned. He wears an extravagant Mexican hat and speaks with an assumed Yankee twang

Aubrey (*to Louise*) Hi, little lady! And whom have I the honour to address?

Louise I'm your cousin Louise Allington.

Aubrey (*taking her hand*) Vibrate that again, sweetie.

Louise I'm your cousin Louise Allington.

Aubrey I'm real glad to meet you socially.

The shake hands

Registered! Do you mind if I mosey? (*He moves into the room through the windows*) Hi, folks. I'm long-lost Cousin George Maitland from Mexico.

Jean turns and sees him for the first time. She is transfixed, staring at him for a moment as if in a great sense of shock. Aubrey stands bemused. Jean recovers and rushes at Aubrey, flings her arms round his neck

Jean Darling ...

She faints in his arms. Louise in a trice realizes the whole situation

Aubrey She's fainted—get some water.

Louise (*to Chesterman*) Get some water!

Chesterman shouting "Water" rushes out through the double doors

Aubrey Quick, what does this mean?
Louise You met her at the station today?

She helps Aubrey during this to put Jean on the settle

Aubrey I know, and she shrieked out: "Darling". So I bolted.
Louise She's George Maitland's wife!
Aubrey George Maitland's wife? You mean George Maitland's *wife*? But what am I to do?
Louise Play up to it—pretend you are her husband. Do what you like, only give me time to think it out. Hush!

Chesterman enters through the double doors with a glass of water

Aubrey (*taking the glass and drinking some of it*) Thank you so much. That's better. She'll be all wife again in a minute.

Under the last, Louise quietly explains the situation to Chesterman

Chesterman (*as he comprehends*) Oh. Oh. A terrible shock, naturally. (*Smiling*) I must congratulate you doubly.
Aubrey Thank you and thank you.
Chesterman You never expected a fortune and a wife on the same day.
Aubrey I didn't.
Chesterman Didn't you?
Aubrey No, I didn't.
Chesterman It's a day you'll never forget.
Aubrey It is.
Jean (*almost revived, faintly*) George ... George ...
Louise (*trying to signal Aubrey*) George ...
Chesterman (*likewise*) George ...
Aubrey (*likewise*) George ... (*Realizing*) Oh, here I am—darling! (*He sits on the settle with her*)
Jean George—George—is it really you?
Aubrey Yes, darling! It's me all right.
Jean Oh, George! (*She throws her arms around his neck. Faintly*) It is really you, George, isn't it?
Aubrey Oh, yes, darling—it's nobody else.
Jean (*gazing at him*) Yes, I'm sure it is.
Aubrey I'm certain of it, too.
Jean George—kiss me.

She closes her eyes expectantly. Aubrey looks to the others. Chesterman looks encouraging, Louise nods approval rather more reluctantly. A long kiss

(*Sighing*) I could have told you anywhere, George, by the way you kiss.

Aubrey, after kissing Jean, appears rather to enjoy the situation

Aubrey It seems almost too good to be true.

Louise is still behind the settle

Louise (*coldly*) It does.

Aubrey Just like a dream, eh?

Louise Oh, you will wake up in a minute.

Jean To think of the years we have lost, George!

Aubrey Oh, I know all about that, darling, think of what lies before us.

Louise (*pointedly*) Yes, I should think of that. (*She moves away rather angrily*)

Jean kisses Aubrey again

Sprules enters through the double doors. The moment he sees Aubrey, he begins making signs—scratching his elbow

Aubrey gazes at Sprules in amazement. At length, Louise also sees Sprules

Sprules, what on earth are you doing?

Sprules Nothing, madam.

Louise Well, don't go on like that, please. I don't like it. What do you want?

Sprules Which room am I to put Mr Maitland in, madam?

Louise The blue room, Sprules—the one next to mine.

Jean (*coyly*) Oh, no, darling, not now! (*Rising*) Hadn't we better tell Sprules that George—that I—oh, help me out, dear. (*She turns away bashfully*)

Louise (*desperately*) Sprules—Mr George Maitland turns out to be—to be Miss Everard's husband . . .

Sprules shows surprise

Yes, it is a surprise to all of us!

Jean (*smiling*) So you see, Sprules, you will take Mr Maitland's things to my room and——

Louise But, Jean, it's only got a—a—(*desperately*)—single—it's quite a small room.

Jean (*sweetly*) Oh, but we shan't mind that, shall we, George?

Aubrey (*cheerfully*) Not a bit—darling. (*He embraces her*) What is enough for one is enough for two!

Louise (*icily*) Oh, of course, if you don't mind . . .

Aubrey As if we should!

Jean That's all right, then, Sprules.

Sprules (*anxiously*) Very good, ma'am.

Sprules moves towards the door making furtive ear signs. Aubrey is very puzzled

Sprules exits reluctantly through the double doors

Jean I think, George, I'll go upstairs—and rest for a little. (*She looks lovingly at him*) Would you like to take me up, darling?

Aubrey Of course I will—dearest!

Louise (*as Aubrey passes*) Oh, I'll pay you out for this.

Jean and Aubrey exit arm in arm through the double doors

Chesterman What a charming picture!

Louise Very!

Chesterman We little knew what we were doing when we brought him down, did we?

Louise We didn't!

Chesterman He's a singularly fascinating man. I can see any woman falling in love with him.

Louise Can you? (*She sits at the tea table and angrily stabs bread and butter into her mouth through the next*)

Chesterman But one can see he's madly in love with her.

Louise Really!

Chesterman Oh, it's obvious! They're just like lovers.

The floor creaks upstairs. The chandelier swings a couple of times, no more. They look up

I'm afraid you'll find it very dull just now, Mrs Allington.

Louise Dull—why?

Chesterman He'll monopolize her altogether now.

Louise (*firmly*) Will he?

Giles enters from the french windows with a basket of gooseberries

Chesterman And you'll have to look on.

Giles Like a gooseberry?

Louise No, thank you, Giles.

Giles The berries are very fine.

Louise (*loudly*) No, nothing, thank you.

Giles All right, 'm.

Giles exits

Louise (*to Chesterman*) You must excuse our gardener coming in here—he's not on speaking terms with Cook.

Chesterman Still, at least you've been the means of bringing two people together. Think how nice it will be for you in the years to come to be able, perhaps, to tell their children that——

Aubrey enters through the double doors

Ah, here is the new bridegroom! Well, Mr Maitland, there's no need to ask if you are happy—your face tells its own tale! Ha, ha!

Aubrey Ha, ha!

Louise (*icily*) Ha, ha!

Chesterman Well, I'm afraid I must be running away. Goodbye, Mrs Allington—(*he shakes hands*)—goodbye, Mr Maitland. (*With a jovial smile*) You're done for this time.

Chesterman exits through the double doors

Aubrey I believe you're right. (*He goes up after Chesterman, closes the doors and returns*)

There is a pause during which Aubrey regards Louise nervously. He attempts, by means of gesture rather than speech, to explain away his behaviour

Louise (*furiously; going to him*) How dare you!

Aubrey retreats

How dare you!

Aubrey retreats further

How dare you!

Aubrey (*sullenly*) I couldn't help myself.

Louise Couldn't help yourself! You had an enormous helping and you enjoyed it——

Aubrey It was your suggestion.

Louise What?

Aubrey You said I was to play it up for all I was worth.

Louise That's right! Now say it's my fault.

Aubrey It is your fault. You made me die, but I didn't want to do it.

Louise How was I to know she was going to turn up?

Aubrey You weren't to know any more than I was. It just happened.

Louise Well, it's got to unhappen!

Aubrey I don't see how. She's got first call on me, in the eyes of the law.

Louise (*startled*) What do you mean?

Aubrey What I say.

Louise I am your lawful wedded wife.

Aubrey (*rising*) Pardon me—you're a corpse's relic. My legal better half is at the present moment reclining on her couch upstairs planning golden dreams for our second honeymoon. 'Ra! 'ra! 'ra!

Louise bursts into tears, lies on the settee and threshes about in an angry frenzy

(*Alarmed and trying to stop her*) Oh, darling, can't you take a joke? A man's got to have some recreation. Come on. You sit up and I'll sit down and we'll talk it over.

They both sit, deep in thought. Aubrey is stumped

Louise Aubrey, I've got an idea.

Aubrey I suppose you want me to die again?

Louise However did you guess?

Aubrey Guess! You've got a mind like a burial service.

Louise Listen, dear! (*She sits closer to Aubrey*) Chesterman was saying this afternoon that at Cousin George's death the money all comes to me.

Aubrey (*amazed*) What?

Louise Yes, it all comes to me.

Aubrey Why the Dickens didn't he say so before?

Louise That's just what I told him. He said he left you a copy of the will.

Aubrey I need never have turned up as George Maitland.

Louise Of course not.

Aubrey Oh! I'm not sure I haven't an action against him—for inciting me to murder myself.

Louise Never mind that! Darling, all you've got to do is to die again.

Aubrey I'm sick of dying.

Louise (*laughing*) You did look so funny, Aubrey, when you dropped in with your face all black.

Aubrey I didn't feel funny!

Louise (*putting her arm round Aubrey*) You will die, darling, won't you, just to please me.

Aubrey (*laughing*) I say—she'll—(*pointing upstairs*)—be a real widow then.

Louise (*laughing*) Serve her right.

Louise and Aubrey burst out laughing and embrace affectionately

Simpson enters through the double doors and stops horror-struck

They spring apart

Aubrey And the animal hugged him just like that. It's a terrible thing the buffalo hug.

Louise What is it, Simpson?

Simpson I was just going to clear away the tea, madam.

Louise You'd like some tea, George?

Aubrey Yes, I'll have a tankard.

Louise Bring some fresh tea, Simpson.

Louise moves away to the windows and stares out, deep in thought. Simpson gives the "elbow" signal to Aubrey who looks first puzzled, then rather alarmed. He turns away towards Louise. In desperation, Simpson throws her tray on the ground. Aubrey and Louise turn sharply

Good gracious, Simpson, what are you doing?

Simpson Beg pardon, ma'am, but it slipped out of my hand.

Louise Well, don't be so careless again.

Simpson goes on her hands and knees to pick up the tray. Louise turns away. Simpson, whilst on her knees—makes frantic "ear" signs to Aubrey who is watching her. Simpson, still on her knees and giving the "ear" sign, works her way up towards the double doors. Aubrey follows her

Simpson exits

Aubrey closes the doors. He looks amazed

Aubrey (*opening the doors again and shouting down the hall after her*) I shot a man in Mexico once for doing that! (*He closes the doors again*) Louise, what's the matter with her? Does she suspect?

Louise I don't think so—why?

Aubrey She was making the most extraordinary signs to me.

Louise Never mind that, let's finish this dying business. Somebody will be here directly.

Aubrey (*sitting*) Well, how am I going to die this time?

Louise I think, darling, you'd better be drowned.

Aubrey looks amazedly at Louise

Yes, I think drowning's the best thing for you. (*Thoughtfully*) You see, your body must never be recovered—that's why I suggest drowning.

Aubrey D'you propose tying a brick round my neck?

Louise Oh, no, that won't be necessary. You can go down to the river to bathe.

Aubrey It's beastly cold for bathing.

Louise I can't help that. Undress in the arbour down by the cedar tree, and plunge into the river.

Aubrey Yes, but what about a costume?

Louise Go in without one!

Aubrey It's not respectable to be drowned with nothing on.

Louise hugs him, amused at this

Sprules's arm comes round the door at this point. He throws three or four trays into the room

Aubrey and Louise, close together, spring apart, alarmed

Louise Good heavens, Sprules, what are you doing?

Sprules I'm so sorry, ma'am. They jumped out of my hands like.

Louise I don't know what's the matter with you all today.

Louise turns away, annoyed. Sprules endeavours by "nose" signs to catch Aubrey's attention. Louise turns round

Pick up that tray and go away.

Sprules picks up the tray. Louise turns away

Sprules continues the "nose" sign until he finally exits through the double doors

Aubrey (*amazed*) There is definitely something the matter with the servants today, Louise.

Louise Never mind! Now where were we?

Aubrey I was in the river—with nothing on.

Louise Oh yes! I'll go and get another suit of yours—and I'll put it in the boathouse there.

Aubrey What for?

Louise Why, that's what you've got to put on when you come out.

Aubrey Oh, I do come out?

Louise After you've gone in, I'll go down to the arbour—and get the clothes you're wearing now—I'll say I've just found them in the arbour and I think something must have happened to you.

Aubrey Yes. You'll probably be right.

Louise (*triumphantly*) Then everybody will at once rush down to the arbour and begin searching for you.

Aubrey Yes.

Louise By that time you'll have swum to the other end, fetched your clothes out of the boathouse, changed comfortably and got away!

Aubrey Who do I appear as next—Lilian Gish?

Louise Anything—what does it matter? Come down as Smith or Jones or Brown, and I'll pass you off as an old friend.

Aubrey Brown.

Louise Right. (*Moving to the door*) I'll go and fetch you some spare clothes for the boathouse. I'll be back in a minute. Don't let anyone near the river. If you see someone going that way, stop them. We don't want a crowd there watching you drown.

Aubrey We don't. I'm not coming up three times just to please them.

Louise goes out through the double doors

Aubrey, alone, patrols up and down

Jean enters from the hall. She has changed her dress

Jean (*playfully*) Bo! It's me again.

Aubrey (*equally playfully*) I guessed it must have been.

Jean (*attempting to stroke Aubrey's beard*) Would you like to take me for a little walk in the garden, George?

Aubrey (*nervously removing her hand*) Oh, I don't know. These afternoons are very treacherous in the morning.

Jean But I'd like to see the river.

Aubrey Oh no, I don't think the river's running today.

Simpson passes by outside the french windows, calling to the ducks

(*Calling*) Hey there, where are you going to? My pretty maid?

Simpson I'm going to feed the ducks, sir.

Aubrey Ducks?

Simpson Yes, sir.

Aubrey Say, would those ducks be river ducks, by any chance?

Simpson Yes, sir.

Aubrey Then I'm afraid I can't allow you to feed them.

Simpson Why not, sir?

Aubrey Why not? Because—the ducks are—the ducks are full up. I have that on good authority. Straight from the horse's beak. What have you got there, anyway?

Simpson Bread, sir.

Aubrey You can't give that to ducks ...

Simpson We always do, sir.

Aubrey That bread's heavy. You give that to ducks and they'll blow right up and—sink.

Simpson (*puzzled*) Really, sir?

Jean (*admiringly*) You're so knowledgeable, George.

Miss Mullett comes through the double doors

Miss Mullett I've told Giles to fetch me a chair.

Jean Miss Mullett, this is my husband, George Maitland.

Miss Mullett (*reacting in alarm at the sight of Aubrey*) No wonder you fainted. Tell Giles I'll be down by the river, Simpson.

Aubrey River? Say, don't go. Stay a while, please.

Miss Mullett Why?
Aubrey I need to talk. I need to talk to you all. Right now. Urgently.
Miss Mullett What about?
Aubrey (*stumped*) I'll think of something.
Jean Perhaps he's going to tell us his adventures.
Miss Mullett His what?
Aubrey My what?
Jean Are you going to tell us about your adventures, George?
Aubrey Er—perhaps possibly.

Giles passes by the windows with a chair

Giles (*as he passes*) Chair.
Aubrey Good man.
Giles I'll put it by the river. (*He moves off*)
Aubrey (*chasing after him*) No, wait! You bring that chair right on in here and sit down, do you hear?
Giles She wanted it by the river.
Aubrey Well, I want it here. I want everyone, I want all of you with all of your chairs in here. Now.
Miss Mullett Better do as he says, I think he's slightly unhinged.

Sprules enters from the hall with Miss Mullett's knitting bag

Aubrey (*seeing him*) That includes you. What do you want?
Sprules Miss Mullett wanted her knitting by the river, sir.
Aubrey (*getting rather desperate*) Well, I don't want no-one knitting in that river, today. Not near those ducks. (*He grabs the knitting bag from Sprules and gives it to Miss Mullett*) Close those doors and sit down.
Sprules Yes, sir. (*He does so*)
Aubrey All of you sit down! Nobody leaves this room till I get a few answers.

They all sit

All right. Let's hear them.

Silence. They all stare at him

Yes. (*Pause*) Yes. (*Pause*) Yes.
Miss Mullett (*impatiently*) Yes?
Jean What sort of weather have you been having in Mexico, George?
Aubrey Thick and clear! (*Reaching the double doors and shouting anxiously into the hall*) Mrs Allington!
Jean Go on, George.
Aubrey (*closing the doors again reluctantly*) Yes, it's an interesting little town, Mexico. Lots of things there. Sombreros. Some don't.

Sprules and Simpson furtively make the "nose" sign at him

(*Mistaking their signal*) Castanets. And—er—mission bells and so on.
Miss Mullett Do people in Mexico go to church on Sundays, Mr Maitland?

Aubrey Oh, yes. Not all that quite often infrequently. Twice sometimes—twice a year.

Miss Mullett What hymns do they use?

Aubrey Oh, any hymns they can get. There's a great shortage.

Miss Mullett Ancient and Modern?

Aubrey Now and again.

Jean Did you ever see any lions, George?

Aubrey Oh—hundreds. Prancing round on the beach there.

Jean Oh, how thrilling!

Aubrey I was once attacked by some.

Sprules and Simpson make the "ear" sign to him

(*Mistaking their sign again and speaking louder*) I say I was once attacked by some . . .

Jean Were you really—how many?

Miss Mullett (*counting her knitting*) Fifteen—sixteen—seventeen—eighteen—nineteen——

Aubrey (*butting in*) Oh, not quite as many as that.

Jean Oh, Miss Mullett—do listen, George was once attacked by lions—he's going to tell us all about it.

Miss Mullett Go on then!

Aubrey Well. (*Dramatically*) I was lying——

Miss Mullett (*to Jean*) I thought as much . . . ?

Aubrey (*glaring at her*) In bed. I was lying in bed when suddenly I awoke with a start. It was as black as ink all around me, but in the open doorway——(*He points first towards the double doors*)

But as he does so Louise opens them, witnesses the scene and closes them again

(*Pointing elsewhere*) No, no, that doorway! I made out two shadowy forms.

Miss Mullett That's why I always keep my door locked.

Aubrey Just at that moment, the clock struck one.

Jean And you struck the other. (*She giggles*)

Aubrey I sprang out of bed—snatched up a gun.

Miss Mullett (*to Jean*) Snatched up a bun?

Aubrey Let fly with both currants—with both barrels—(*pause*)—when I struck a match, they were all three of them dead—both of them.

Jean Dead?

Aubrey Yes. They've been dead for years.

A dramatic pause

Louise steals past outside the french windows with a bundle of clothes. She waves to Aubrey to keep going

Miss Mullett What made you keep barrels of currants in your hotel?

Aubrey (*very heavily*) Hotels! Woman, we've got no hotels out there. We lived in barrels, way up on the plains—down on the—sugar loaf mountains—we were just a bunch of wild mice frightened to death—(*pause*)—of cats.

Miss Mullett I don't wonder. I should be wild if I had to live on currants.

Jean Go on, George . . . Were you ever taken prisoner by Indians?

Aubrey Er—yes. As a matter of fact, I was—once taken prisoner by Indians—as it happens. Once.

Miss Mullett (*suspiciously*) Were you?

Aubrey Punjabs.

Miss Mullett Why did they let you go again?

A silence. Aubrey puzzles on this

Simpson (*who has become absorbed in the tale, trying to be helpful*) He escaped.

Jean (*seizing on this*) George escaped. Didn't you, George?

Aubrey I escaped.

Miss Mullett How?

Aubrey (*desperately*) I—er—swam away.

Miss Mullett Oh, it was an island, then?

Aubrey (*obviously uncomfortable*) Oh, yes, it was an island.

Miss Mullett I didn't know they had islands in Mexico.

Aubrey (*irritably*) Have you ever been to Mexico?

Miss Mullett Certainly not.

Aubrey Then they do. They've had 'em for years. Little ones—with water all round them. Which I swimmed. Swam.

Miss Mullett Why didn't you take a boat?

Pause

Giles (*helpfully*) There weren't no boats there.

Jean (*helpfully*) There probably weren't any boats there.

Aubrey There weren't no boats there.

Miss Mullett Then how did the Indians get you across in the first place?

Pause. Everyone is stumped by this one, including Aubrey

Louise arrives back through the french windows, somewhat breathless, having disposed of the bundle of clothes

Miss Mullett Well?

Jean Well, George?

Miss Mullett How did the Indians get you across?

Louise Cousin George! Surely you're not going to forget your promise?

Aubrey (*startled*) Sorry?

Miss Mullett What promise?

Louise George promised he wouldn't tell. Didn't you George?

Aubrey That's it. I promised I wouldn't tell. On pain of drowning.

Louise If you would like to have a pipe in the garden, Cousin George, don't let us stop you.

Aubrey Think I will. Talking of drowning, that river of yours looks mighty small and tempting, Mrs Allington. Reminds me of dear old Mississippi before she was married. See you in the river.

Miss Mullett rises angrily and heads for the double doors

Louise Where are you going, Auntie?
Miss Mullett To get some more wool.
Louise Oh, right.
Miss Mullett (*as she disappears*) And a pinch of salt.

Simpson and Sprules have opened the doors for her and now follow her out

Giles is still seated on his chair

Louise That will do, Giles. You can put that chair back and tidy the potting shed.
Giles Yes, 'm. I reckon they carried him across at low tide on their 'eads, those Indians. Like that. (*He demonstrates*)
Louise Yes, thank you, Giles.

Giles goes off into the garden with the chair

Jean I think I'll go and watch George swim.
Louise (*hurriedly*) Oh, Jean, don't go for a minute. I want to talk to you about something frightfully, frightfully, frightfully important.

She seats Jean and then sits herself. A slight pause

Jean (*sitting again*) Well, dear? What is it?

Louise goes over and closes the french windows

Louise You don't mind if I close the windows, do you? I'm feeling a little chilly.

Louise closes the french windows, glancing anxiously out as she does so. She sits again elsewhere, looks about to speak, then rises abruptly. She goes to the windows, then sits again in a third chair

Jean You're not worried about anything, are you, Louise?
Louise Oh no, dear, not at all.
Jean I'm glad of that. For my part—I shall never forget today!
Louise I don't think I shall either.

Unseen by them, Simpson hurries past outside the french windows in the direction of the arbour

Jean You don't know how grateful I am to you, Louise! But for you this would never have happened.
Louise No . . .

Sprules enters through the double doors. As he does so, Giles crosses the garden towards the river with an oar from the potting shed

Sprules Shall I clear away tea, madam?
Louise Yes, Sprules. Do you know if Miss Mullett found her wool?
Sprules It was not in her room, so she sent Simpson on a comprehensive search for it, madam.

Sprules exits with the tray with tea things through the double doors

Simpson passes the french windows with the suit of clothes

Louise Why, Simpson, what have you got there?

Simpson I found them in the arbour, madam.

Louise Oh, Simpson, you shouldn't have moved them. They're Mr Maitland's clothes. He's gone swimming.

Jean Oh, dear . . .

Simpson Sorry, madam.

Louise (*to Jean*) It's all right, dear, I'll have them taken back . . . Simpson, take them back at once.

Simpson Yes, madam . . .

Jean Oh no, dear. Not Simpson, surely. Not if he's——

Louise What?

Jean Not if he's swimming in the—without his . . .

Simpson giggles

Louise Oh. No, of course. Give them here, Simpson.

Sprules enters through the double doors

(*Taking the clothes*) Sprules, run down to the arbour with these clothes, quickly, they belong to Mr Maitland. He's gone for a swim. (*She hands Sprules the clothes*)

Sprules Yes, ma'am. (*In sudden alarm*) A swim, ma'am?

Louise Yes, a swim.

Sprules But he can't swim, ma'am.

Jean Yes, he can.

Louise Yes, he can, Sprules. Now hurry.

Sprules (*flustered and alarmed*) Very good, ma'am.

He goes off hurriedly through the french windows with the clothes

Miss Mullett enters through the double doors, seeing him

Miss Mullett Where is he going with those clothes?

Louise We're sending him back to the arbour with them, Auntie.

Miss Mullett Why?

Jean Because they are my husband's, Miss Mullett.

Miss Mullett Well, shouldn't he have them on? It's normal, even for a lunatic.

Louise But he's gone for a swim, Auntie.

Miss Mullett Oh, I see. Indians chasing him again, are they?

Miss Mullett goes out through the double doors

Sprules enters hurriedly through the french windows, still with the clothes

Sprules I can see the whole of the reach of the river from the lawn, but there's no sign of Mr Maitland anywhere.

All turn to him

Jean What!

Louise Jean! He might have got cramp. I remember, he had it once when we were—he could have got cramp. Men do. Often. When they're—swimming. (*She stops, confused*)

Jean Good heavens! Suppose something's happened to him! George! George!

She rushes out through the french windows

Louise follows her a little. Sprules, the clothes still in his arms, stands stunned. Simpson, who has been hovering anxiously in the background, moves to him

Simpson (*softly*) Oh, Mr Sprules ...

Sprules (*in a low tone, grief-stricken*) Henery ... Henery.

Sprules throws the clothes on the ground and rushes out through the double doors; Simpson follows him

(*Off, a great cry from the hallway*) HENERY ...

Louise returns to the room pleased and relieved

Louise (*sitting*) It's all right! It's all right! (*She does a little dance with glee*)

Giles passes the french windows, carrying a bundle of clothes

Giles Clothes!

Louise (*vaguely*) What's that?

Giles Found them in the boathouse.

Louise (*rising*) You—you—found them in the boathouse?

Giles Nice suit of clothes, too!

Louise Oh, my heavens, you've ruined everything.

Giles Anything wrong?

Louise Wrong? Everything's wrong. He's got no clothes at all now. Oh, you idiot, you imbecile. Here—give them to me! (*She snatches the clothes and moves to the windows*)

Giles (*making to follow her*) I'll go and see if there are any more there.

Louise No, no! Anywhere but that. Go to the kitchen.

Giles The kitchen? What about Cook?

Louise Oh, hang Cook.

Giles Very good, mum.

Giles exits through the double doors

Louise (*despairingly*) Oh, Aubrey! Aubrey!

Louise stands for a second undecided. Finally, she shrugs, tosses the bundle into the air and sits. As she does so:

Aubrey enters through the french windows. He is practically naked, soaking wet and covered in duckweed. He has managed to find a couple of boat cushions which he clasps to him to preserve his modesty. He opens his mouth and spouts water. As he stands dripping in the doorway—

the CURTAIN *falls*

ACT III

The same. The following day. Late afternoon

As the CURTAIN *goes up Sprules is seated deep in gloom. Simpson is searching for something. The double doors are open to the hall*

Simpson You can say what you like, Mr Sprules—there's a fatality haunting this house.

Sprules There is something unlucky about it.

Simpson Unlucky! I should say so. First the master gets exploded. Then your brother gets drowned, and now I've gone and lost my best brooch.

Sprules Well, let's hope that's the finish of it, anyway. Poor old 'Enery, fancy his being drowned; still I'm not sure that it isn't all for the best.

Simpson Why, Mr Sprules?

Sprules (*contemptuously*) Why, did you notice the way he was carrying on with that Miss Everard—Mrs Maitland—whatever she calls 'erself.

Simpson I should think I did.

Sprules Another two days of that, and he'd have forgotten what he came down here for. But then I told you, didn't I say—'Enery always was a fool where ladies were concerned?

Simpson And 'im a married man too.

Sprules That's not his fault, it's his nature. I always said 'Enery would have made a faithful husband to any woman, providing he was married to someone else.

Simpson He was on the stage, wasn't he?

Sprules Yes, scene shifter.

Simpson I thought as much—he clicked with her all right.

Sprules Yes, she seemed to make him clean balmy. I passed him on the stairs yesterday, as he was taking her up to her room, and I whispered——

Simpson "How are you going?"

Sprules "How are you going?"—then gave him the sign—(*he demonstrates the "nose" sign*)——

Simpson copies him

Don't make that noise!—why, he stared at me as if I was mad.

Simpson His mind wasn't on his work—look at him over the tray. I dented it in three places, trying to attract his attention.

Sprules (*gloomily*) A lot of notice he took, didn't he?

Simpson What I wants to know is what's going to happen if they find his body. They'll know in a moment then who he is.

40   Tons of Money

Sprules Let's hope they don't find it. I shall never forget yesterday afternoon, as long as I live.

Simpson More shall I. When she heard your brother was drowned——

Sprules (*with her*)—drowned——

Simpson —that Miss Everard goes off into hysterics——

Sprules (*with her*)—hysterics——

Simpson —because she's lost her husband.

Sprules (*with her*) Husband. Then Chesterman rings up to say he was a fraud——

Simpson (*with him*)—fraud——

Sprules —and the real George Maitland——

Simpson (*with him*)—Maitland——

Sprules —himself's coming down today——

Simpson (*with him*)—today——

Sprules
Simpson } (*together*)—so she has another go of hysterics.

Simpson Oh, if only you'd known he was coming, Mr Sprules, you'd have saved your brother's life!

Sprules Don't rub it in. (*He takes a handkerchief from his inside pocket and starts to cry*) It's bad enough to think he's drowned, without remembering each time that I sort of lead him into it . . . (*He cries*)

Simpson comes to him and tries to soothe him. The doorbell is heard, off

Look out, this is probably him.

Both move to the double doors

At the last moment, Sprules is overcome with a fresh bout of grief and runs off into the garden

Simpson Mr Sprules——!

The doorbell rings again

Simpson rather tearfully goes to answer it herself. In a moment, she ushers in Henery, disguised as George Maitland. He is wearing a suit, and carries a hat. He appears a little ill at ease

(*Inaudibly through her sobs*) Mrs Allington will be with you directly, sir.

She goes before Henery can hand her his hat, closing the double doors behind her

Henery stands awkwardly

Sprules hurries past the french windows blowing his nose

Henery moves to follow him, vainly making the "ear" and "nose" signs to Sprules' retreating back

Louise enters through the double doors. She doesn't immediately see Henery and braces herself for the interview

Henery turns and does likewise

Louise (*going to greet him*) Cousin George ...

Henery (*shaking her hand*) Mrs Allington?

Louise You can imagine how amazed I was when Mr Chesterman rang to say you were coming.

Henery He is the lawyer man, isn't he?

Louise Yes, I expect him here this afternoon to meet you. You really were the last person we ... such a nice surprise ... We've had some rather curious things happening lately, Mr Maitland.

Miss Mullett wanders in through the french windows during this, searching for something as usual and taking no notice of the other occupants of the room

Henery stares uncertainly at her

Henery Have there?

Louise Yes, you see, yesterday we had this man arrive who——(*She breaks off as she sees Miss Mullett*)

Miss Mullett (*muttering, as to herself*) Where did I put it? Do you know where I put it?

Henery (*feeling he should answer*) I couldn't tell you.

Miss Mullett (*startled to see him there*) What!

Louise Oh, Auntie, let me introduce you to Mr George Maitland—my aunt, Miss Mullett.

Henery How-do-you-do, Miss Mullett, how-do-you-do? Delighted to meet you, I'm sure.

Miss Mullett (*without paying him much attention, beyond an initial suspicious glance*) I suppose he really is George Maitland?

Henery (*startled, in his normal voice*) Er—of course I am. Who do you think I am?

Louise Well, we had another one here yesterday.

Henery What?

Louise I thought that would surprise you.

Henery Where—where is he?

Miss Mullett He's drowned.

Henery (*horrified*) Drowned?

Louise He was evidently a very clever impostor.

Miss Mullett He was a blackguard.

Louise Oh, Auntie!

Miss Mullett An absolute blackguard.

Henery Well, what do you think of that!

Louise Do sit down. Of course now we've got you here, Cousin George, it's all right.

Henery (*sitting down, rather relieved*) Yes, of course, but it naturally surprised a chap a bit, what?

Louise He did it very cleverly, you know. He deceived us all.

Miss Mullett Yes, including your wife, Mr Maitland.

Henery (*amazed*) My—which?

Miss Mullett Your wife!

Henery is regarding them with horror. Miss Mullett finding her knitting, now sits and continues with it

Louise Of course, you didn't know your wife was here!
Henery Er—er—no! I didn't!
Miss Mullett Another little surprise for you.
Louise I wonder where she is. (*She rings the bell*)
Henery (*helplessly*) What's she like?
Miss Mullett What?
Henery Is she like what she was like—I mean—has she altered much?
Louise No, I don't think so—why?
Henery (*eagerly*) I have, you know—an awful lot.
Louise It's a shame you couldn't have found time to write to her, Mr Maitland. We'd all given you up for . . . lost.
Henery I can't—much write—in Mexico. Write much. (*He flounders for words*)

Sprules enters through the double doors

Henery vainly endeavours by means of signs to attract his attention

Louise Sprules, where is Mrs Maitland?
Sprules In the garden, ma'am.
Louise Tell her that Mr Maitland is here.
Sprules Yes, ma'am.

Sprules exits into the garden through the french windows

Henery Shall I go and help find her?
Louise Oh, no. Do sit down. Sprules will tell her.
Henery You know, I expect I'm awfully changed since she last saw me.
Louise So you were saying.
Miss Mullett Love can penetrate any disguise.
Henery (*in his own voice*) That's what I was thinking. (*As Maitland*) It's just that she may get a bit of a surprise when she sees me.
Miss Mullett (*looking at him critically*) I don't doubt she will.

Jean enters from the garden

Louise Ah, here she is!
Jean (*not believing her eyes*) George—George—is it really you?
Henery (*nervously*) Yes, darling. It's me all right.
Jean (*going to Henery*) Oh, George! (*She falls into his arms and swoons*)
Henery She's fainted.
Louise Here we go again . . .

She helps Henery to carry Jean to the sofa

Jean (*drowsily*) It is really you, George, isn't it?
Henery Oh yes, darling, it's nobody else.
Jean (*gazing at Henery*) Yes, I'm sure it is.
Henery I'm certain of it too.
Jean George, you can kiss me.

Henery looks nervous

Miss Mullett You needn't mind us.

Jean and Henery kiss

Jean (*sighing*) I could have told you anywhere, George, by the way you kiss. (*She sits close to Henery*) You've been away such a long time, darling.

Henery starts to kiss Jean again

Miss Mullett (*interrupting this*) I understood you were shot, Mr Maitland.
Henery (*startled*) Shot!
Jean Yes, darling, in Mexico.
Louise In a saloon.
Jean Where were you wounded, George?
Henery In the saloon—I forget.
Miss Mullett Forgot?
Jean Your friend wrote and said you risked your life for another.
Henery (*bravely*) Oh, it's nothing. We do that every day in Nevada.
Jean Nevada?
Louise What were you doing in Nevada?
Henery I went there for a weekend.
Miss Mullett It's miles away from Mexico, Nevada.
Henery Ah, well. That's the point. We never got there, did we?
Jean You didn't?
Miss Mullett So were you shot or weren't you, Mr Maitland?
Henery Oh, I was shot all right, but it wasn't that serious, you know.
Jean But if it wasn't serious, George, why have you never written?
Henery Well, dear, there was this great . . . shortage of stamps.
Jean (*tearfully*) You've been away so long, George.
Henery Oh, ten years is nothing in Mexico.
Jean Ten! It's not five since you left England.
Henery It's seemed like ten, dearest.

Pause. Henery is obviously nervous

Jean You must have had some adventures since you left England, George?
Henery Oh, yes. Amazing.
Miss Mullett (*quickly*) Tell us some.
Henery Ah.
Jean Oh, do, George! We should simply love to hear them.
Miss Mullett Ever taken prisoner by Indians?
Henery Er—no, I don't think so.
Miss Mullett The other George Maitland was.
Louise But he was an impostor, Auntie.
Miss Mullett All men are! My dear mother used to say: "Show me a man and I'll show you Beelzebub".
Jean (*confidentially to Henery*) George darling, d'you remember . . . .do you remember the pet name you always used to call me?
Henery Do I remember it? As if I could ever forget! Er—let me see now— what was it again?

Jean (*coyly*) Little Blossom!
Miss Mullett Little Fossil?
Louise Blossom, Auntie!
Miss Mullett When I was a girl I was called Fudge. I can't think why.

Sprules enters through the double doors

Sprules Mr Chesterman to see you, ma'am.

Louise rises

> *Chesterman enters through the double doors*
>
> *Sprules exits through the double doors*

Chesterman Ah, how-do-you-do, Mrs Allington? (*He shakes hands with her*)
Louise How are you, Mr Chesterman? You know everyone, I think?

Chesterman bows all round, then stares at Henery

Oh, this is Mr George Maitland.

Chesterman crosses to Henery and shakes hands

Chesterman This is the George Maitland at last, I hope?
Henery Of course I am. Who do you think I am?
Chesterman Well, you can hardly blame me for asking, Mr Maitland. We had an impostor here yesterday.
Henery Yes, so I've 'eard—(*he coughs*)—heard.
Chesterman And—(*to Louise*) if I understood you correctly on the telephone this morning, Mrs Allington—he was drowned, you say?
Jean We found his clothes, but his body has never been recovered.
Chesterman What an amazing thing!
Henery (*jocularly*) P'raps he heard I'd turned up—and got nervous.
Jean That's what I believe.
Chesterman I wonder who he was.
Louise I can't think!
Miss Mullett Well, the body's sure to be recovered, and then we shall know.
Chesterman When did you arrive in England, Mr Maitland?
Henery Er—last—yesterday.
Jean Oh, if only you'd come down then, George!
Chesterman (*laughing*) It would have been funny, wouldn't it?
Louise It would, indeed!
Henery You got my telegram all right, Mr Cheeseman.
Jean Chesterman, dear.
Chesterman Yes, thank you, Mr Maitland, but why did you send two?
Henery I didn't.
Chesterman Oh, but you did—I had them within an hour of each other.

Pause, during which they all look at Henery

Jean Why did you send two, George?

Chesterman has produced two telegrams

Chesterman One handed in at Piccadilly: (*reading*) "Just arrived in England. Going to Marlow tomorrow. Maitland." The other was handed in at Liverpool: "Just arrived in England, expect me tomorrow."

Jean (*helpfully*) Perhaps you forgot, George?

Henery Yes—that's it—er—I must have forgot all about it. I'm terribly absent-minded. (*A thought suddenly occurs to him*) I lost my memory once in Mexico.

Miss Mullett (*to Louise*) What did he lose, dear?

Louise His memory, Auntie.

Miss Mullett Oh, I thought it might have been something valuable.

Henery It was a horrible experience, Mrs Muffett.

Miss Mullett (*annoyed*) What was?

Henery The time I lost my memory.

Miss Mullett How did you find it again?

Henery Oh, it—er—sort of came back—quite suddenly. I often do it now, you know. It simply goes—and when I come to myself, it's gone and I don't remember anything about it.

Miss Mullett Nothing at all?

Henery No, absolutely nothing.

Miss Mullett (*calmly*) Then, how do you know you've ever lost it?

Henery regards Jean helplessly for a moment

Henery (*with a stroke of inspiration*) Where am I?

Jean Why, obviously, Miss Mullett, someone tells him of the extraordinary things he has done.

Henery (*quickly*) That's it! That's it! And then, you see, I just jump to the conclusion at once.

Miss Mullett Decidedly interesting!

Henery (*feeling more at ease*) I've told you this just in case, I don't say I shall, you know—but just in case I should say or do extraordinary things here.

Miss Mullett You probably will. The other one did.

Jean But if you did, darling, is there no way to bring you round?

Louise We certainly ought to know.

Henery Well, you mustn't worry me at all with questions, that's the worst thing you can do. Just—er—humour me——

Jean strokes his beard

—and if it gets very bad—(*nervously removing Jean's hands from his beard*)—please leave that alone, dearest——

Jean (*disappointed*) Oh . . .

Henery —let me sleep it off.

Louise Let you sleep it off?

Henery That's it, that's it.

Jean I'm glad you've told us, dear, we won't forget.

Louise Soothe you and humour you, and let you sleep it off.

Henery (*emphatically*) And, of course, never refer to it again.

Sprules enters through the double doors

Sprules A Brother Brown to see you, ma'am.
Louise Brother Brown? (*Realizing*) Oh, Brother *Brown* . . .
Sprules He's a monk, madam.
Louise Show him in, Sprules.

Sprules exits through the double doors

Miss Mullett When I was a girl I used to love monks.

Sprules enters again

Sprules Brother Brown.

Aubrey enters. He is disguised as a monk, in full habit, sandals, tonsure and carrying a thick, rustic staff

Sprules exits

Aubrey Ah, my dear Louise, this is indeed a pleasure—I suppose I can take the privilege of an old friend . . . (*He shakes hands and kisses Louise*)
Louise Oh, my dear Brother Brown, how do you do—I haven't seen you for years.
Aubrey And you haven't beaten a retreat lately either have you, you naughty girl!
Louise Let me introduce you, Brother Brown—Miss Mullett, Mrs Maitland, Mr Chesterman.

Aubrey greets them all in turn

(*After a pause, turning to Henery*) And this, Brawberry—Brother—(*nervously*)—is Mr George Maitland.
Aubrey (*in his natural voice*) What! (*Assuming his other voice quickly*) And what the hel——hello, who may you be—doing here?—what may you be doing here?
Louise (*deliberately*) Mr Maitland, Brother Brown, has only just turned up most unexpectedly from Mexico.
Henery Yes, owing to Aubrey Allington's death . . .

Aubrey, who has difficulty understanding Henery's accent throughout looks to Louise

Louise (*interpreting for him*) Owing to Aubrey Allington's death . . .
Aubrey A most lamentable occurrence.
Jean You knew him, Brother Brown?
Aubrey Oh, most intimately. He and I were—like this.
Henery He was a top-hole chap, I've heard.

Aubrey looks puzzled again

Louise (*interpreting for him again*) He was a top-hole chap . . .
Aubrey A noble soul, Mr Maitland. Too good for this wicked world.
Louise (*tearfully*) Everybody loved him.

Aubrey How could they help it? Ah me! Here tomorrow and gone this afternoon.

Jean You would scarcely credit it, Brother Brown, but we have had an impostor down here trying to palm himself off as George Maitland.

Aubrey (*shaking his head*) Dear! Dear! Dear! Dear! Dear! Dear! You fill me with incredulity.

Jean Something warned me he was an impostor directly I saw him.

Aubrey How utterly wonderful is woman's instinct. (*With a look at Louise*) One can always rely on her for a bright idea, can't one? Where is this fellow now?

Chesterman He was drowned yesterday.

Miss Mullett Why have you got four of them?

Aubrey (*startled*) What!

Miss Mullett (*loudly*) I said why have you got four knots. In your belt. I thought you were only supposed to have three? Poverty, Chastity and Obedience. What's your other one knot for?

Aubrey (*stumped for a moment*) Er—that's—that one's—to remind me not to forget the other three.

Miss Mullett Extraordinary.

Aubrey (*returning to the subject, hastily*) Have you—have you any idea as to who he was? This unfortunate fellow in the lake?

Louise Not the remotest.

Aubrey (*relieved, relaxing into his natural voice*) That's all right—(*pulling himself up*)—I mean, it will be all right when they find the body.

Chesterman (*to Louise*) Did he go out intending to bathe?

Jean No, it seems that the idea must have suddenly struck him. He apparently just took off his clothes and went in.

Aubrey And forgot to come out, I suppose?

Jean
Louise } (*together*) Mmmm . . .
Chesterman
Henery

They muse on this

Miss Mullett When I was a girl we always wore costumes.

Aubrey (*very earnestly looking at Miss Mullett*) I hope so.

Miss Mullett rises suddenly and abruptly and moves to the french windows. People are startled

Louise Where are you going, Auntie?

Miss Mullett I'm going to take a quick turn around the lake before dinner. See if he's floated to the surface.

Miss Mullett goes off into the garden

Jean George dear, would you like to take me for a little stroll?

Henery Oh, all right, dearest.

Jean Just the two of us?

Henery (*warming to the idea*) Oh, yes . . .

Jean (*playfully pushing him*) That's if you can catch me first!

With a peal of girlish laughter she rushes out into the garden. Henery looks at the others rather sheepishly then runs after Jean. They pursue each other playfully in the garden

Chesterman What a singularly fascinating man. I can see any woman falling in love with him. (*He goes to the french windows and watches them*)

Aubrey (*in an undertone, from Chesterman*) Louise, what on earth does this mean?

Louise It's Cousin George Maitland turned up unexpectedly.

Aubrey I know! I can see that!

Louise He wasn't dead.

Aubrey Why not? Why on earth isn't he dead?

Louise Ssssh! It's not my fault, Aubrey, I can't kill everybody.

Aubrey When did he turn up?

Louise Five minutes after you left yesterday, Chesterman rang up about it. And then Maitland himself came along today.

Aubrey It's positively disgusting.

Louise Just when we'd got everything fixed, too.

Aubrey And now he is going to get all our money.

Louise I suppose so!

Aubrey Oh, there must be some way out. There always is. I've a nasty feeling we're in need of another of your ideas.

Louise Well, I haven't got one. Not at the moment.

From the garden, Jean chases past the windows and off towards the river with shrill giggles

Aubrey I know she's your best friend, darling, and I shouldn't really say this but that woman has the brain of a very, very small potted shrimp.

Henery rushes past the windows and off in pursuit of Jean

Chesterman (*returning through the french windows to his briefcase*) Well, thank goodness we've found the real George Maitland at last! There can be no more complications now.

Now the real George Maitland appears at the french windows from the other direction

The others do not see him, and continue their conversation. He is an exact double of Henery, dressed just like him except he wears a single-breasted suit

Maitland Pardon me ...

All register his apparent reappearance without much interest

Louise I thought you'd gone!

Maitland Gone! I've just come, I want to see Mrs Allington.

Aubrey As my brother bellringer would say—pull the other one.

Maitland I'm afraid I don't understand you. I'm George Maitland ... (*He proffers a hand to Aubrey*)

Aubrey (*ignoring his hand*) Yes, yes, of course, we know all about that. But what is the game?

Maitland Game! There's no game. I'm George Maitland of Mexico ... (*He proffers his hand to Chesterman*)

Chesterman (*similarly ignoring him*) Don't keep harping on it, my dear fellow. We know that.

Bewildered, Maitland finally goes to greet Louise

Maitland I'm George Maitland of Mexico.

Louise (*not responding either*) Why aren't you with your wife?

Maitland My wife! (*He laughs in ridicule, and moves away*)

Chesterman, Aubrey and Louise all look at each other in amazement

Louise (*sotto: to the others*) Don't you see? He's lost his memory again.

Chesterman (*sotto*) Of course. It never occurred to me.

Aubrey (*sotto*) How truly sad.

Maitland I couldn't get any sense out of your butler, so I just walked right in.

Louise Yes, yes! (*Aside to the others*) Humour him!

Chesterman
Aubrey } (*together*) Yes, yes!

Maitland I'm George Maitland from Mexico ...

Chesterman
Aubrey } (*together*) Yes, yes!
Louise

Maitland And I've just come down to see a Mr Chesterman ...

Chesterman
Aubrey } (*together*) Yes, yes!
Louise

Louise (*aside*) Keep it up!

Maitland I sent him a wire yesterday ...

Chesterman } (*together*) Yes, yes!
Aubrey

Maitland Don't keep saying "Yes, yes!"

Aubrey No, no!

Maitland (*angrily*) Have you all gone crazy?

Aubrey Yes, yes!

Chesterman No, no!

Maitland Well, you've got me beat!

Louise (*aloud, advancing to Maitland*) You know me, Mr Maitland, don't you?

Maitland Madam, I do not!

Aubrey (*to Chesterman*) Sad! Sad!

Maitland (*turning on Aubrey, angrily*) Say, what's this stuff you're handing me?

Aubrey Nothing, nothing.

Louise I'm Louise, George. Louise Allington—poor dear Aubrey's wife.

Maitland Oh, you're Louise Allington, are you?

Chesterman (*to Aubrey*) He's coming to!

Louise (*taking one of Maitland's hands and starting to pat it*) How are you, Cousin George?

Maitland Well, I shall be all right as soon as I can get anyone to talk sense.

Aubrey Yes, yes.

Maitland (*getting rattled and turning on Aubrey*) Cut that out!

Louise Now, Cousin George, come and sit down. (*Holding his hands, she leads him to a chair*)

Maitland I don't want to sit down. (*He snatches his hands away*)

At this moment, Jean enters from the garden through the french windows, apparently still playing her game of hide and seek with Henery. She stops short, puzzled as she sees Maitland

He, in turn, expresses amazement at seeing her

Jean!!

Jean Oh! How did you get there?

Maitland More important how did you get here?

Jean (*confused*) I——

Chesterman (*to Jean, aside*) Memory's gone.

Aubrey (*to Jean, aside*) Humour him!

Maitland Aren't you pleased to see me?

Jean (*aside*) The poor dear! Yes, George darling. Of course I'm delighted to see you! There, there!

Aubrey
Chesterman } (*together*) There, there!

Maitland (*to Jean*) What in tarnation are you doing here?

Aubrey Here, here!

Jean (*smiling*) Well—I—er—I've just come here to be with you.

Maitland What! You knew I was coming?

Jean Well, not exactly—but—er—why worry about it? Here we are.

Maitland This has got my head flappin' like a whip o' will.

Jean (*soothingly*) Yes, of course.

Louise (*aside*) He is bad this time.

Aubrey (*aside*) Bad, bad …

Maitland (*savagely to Aubrey*) Look for the last time, I'm warning you …

Aubrey (*alarmed*) No offence. Fence.

Jean (*to the others*) Just leave him to me. I'll soon bring him round.

Louise Soothe him and humour him and let him sleep it off.

Jean That's right. I'll get him to sleep.

She ushers Louise, Aubrey and Chesterman to the double doors. Maitland watches suspiciously

Aubrey (*to Jean*) Engage him in conversation. That should send him to sleep.

They exit

Jean closes the double doors. She returns to Maitland

Maitland Now, Jean, for the love of Mike, put me wise. What's the dope they are trying to hand me?

Jean Oh, it's nothing, dear. It's only their little way. (*She gets behind his chair and starts to stroke his beard*)

Maitland The joint is like a madhouse!

Jean Yes, dear, I know. (*Continuing to massage, cooingly*) It's all right, darling. It's all right!

Maitland It isn't all right. Even the butler's plumb loco. When I arrived at the front door and asked if anyone was in he just laughed in my face.

Jean (*soothingly*) So what did you do?

Maitland Do? I gave him my name and told him to announce me.

Jean (*humouring him*) And did he?

Maitland No, he did not. He stared at me and said: "You'd better 'op it quick, the real one's here."

Jean What a thing to say!

Maitland Then he slammed the front door in my face. Here am I, travelling all night, absolutely all in . . .

Jean You want a good rest, darling. Now just make yourself comfortable. Put your feet up——

He does so. Jean helps him. She hums a little of "Ta-ra-ra-boom-de-ay" which causes Maitland to relax a little and smile

——and I'll give orders you're not to be disturbed. (*She moves to the double doors*)

Maitland If that mad monk comes in again I'll wring his neck.

Jean (*at the doors*) I'll see you're not disturbed, darling.

She exits quietly through the double doors, closing them

After she has gone, Maitland sits up and looks round, frowning. Something isn't right. After a moment, he rises and stands thinking, humming the tune in a menacing way. He goes to the double doors and whips them open. There is nobody in the hall

As he does so, Henery comes past the french windows from the direction of the lake. He looks briefly into the room gives a little whistle in case Jean is there but, seeing it apparently empty, continues in the other direction

Maitland, hearing the whistle, closes the double doors and moves towards the french windows, swiftly. As he reaches them . . .

Miss Mullett comes into view, returning from her walk. Maitland steps aside to let her enter. Absorbed as usual in her own thoughts she passes him without noticing him

Maitland Hallo there. I'm George Maitland.

Miss Mullett What!

Maitland George Maitland. I am.

Miss Mullett I know that. Who did you think you were? (*She moves to the double doors*)

Maitland (*bewildered*) What?

Miss Mullett (*at the double doors*) I've just had a thorough look at the lake.
Maitland Oh, yes?
Miss Mullett No sign of a dead body, anywhere.
Maitland What?
Miss Mullett Look for yourself.

Miss Mullett goes out through the double doors, closing them

*Maitland is thoroughly startled. He looks first after Miss Mullett then
out towards the lake. After a moment he hurries into the garden*

*As he disappears, Henery runs on from the other direction. He springs into
the room giving his gorilla imitation, expecting Jean to be there. She isn't.
He tails off rather limply*

Henery Cor, stone the crows what a caper, eh? (*He lies on the sofa to recover
his breath*)

*The double doors open cautiously. Jean enters followed by the others. They
are all singing softly*

Henery is very startled. He leaps to his feet

Jean Oh you're awake!
Henery Awake?
Louise How are you, Cousin George?
Jean How are you feeling now, dear?
Henery Oh, I'm top-hole. I've been looking for you, Little Possum.
Jean Blossom.
Henery Blossom.
Chesterman (*to Louise*) He remembers nothing about it.
Aubrey He's even forgotten her name.
Henery (*turning, looking suspiciously at them*) What are you looking at me
   like that for? What's the matter with me?
Jean (*to Henery*) Nothing, dear, nothing.
Louise He's not quite right yet.
Jean If I were you, darling, I should sit down and rest a little bit. Now, put
   your feet up. (*She helps him put his feet up*)
Aubrey Take the weight off your beard. (*To Louise*) Any ideas yet?
Louise Soothe him and humour him and let him sleep it off. (*To Aubrey*)
   Not a single one.

*Jean signs to the others, who go out through the windows quietly. Louise and
Chesterman stand watching*

Aubrey goes off momentarily in search of Giles

Now you can lie here quietly and go to sleep.
Henery What the deuce do I want to go to sleep for?
Jean Better soon. There, there.

*She starts to stroke his beard, gently humming "Ta-ra-ra-boom-de-ay".
Henery snatches her hands away*

Henery Don't touch that thing!
Jean (*startled*) No, dear!
Henery I told you, I don't like it.
Jean I thought you did.
Henery Well, I don't. Often. Usually. Not today.
Jean (*moving to the windows*) No, dearest. I'll see you're not disturbed.

Jean goes quietly through the french windows, closing them slightly

(*To Louise and Chesterman*) He'll be all right in a little while, I'm sure.

Aubrey joins them, accompanied by Giles

Aubrey In case he shows fight, I've got Giles standing by with a pitchfork.

*Jean closes the windows completely. We can no longer hear their voices.
They take a last look at Henery through the windows and creep away into
the garden*

*After a second, Henery sits up. He very cautiously rises and tiptoes across the
room to the bellpull. He deliberates for a moment, then decides against using
it. He moves to the double doors and opens them cautiously*

Miss Mullett enters

Miss Mullett (*with a nod to Henery as she passes him*) Back again. Take a
look, did you?
Henery (*startled*) Sorry?
Miss Mullett Men float face up, women float face down. Or is it the other
way round? Did you know that?
Henery (*baffled*) No, I didn't.
Miss Mullett There's probably a reason for it but I don't think we want to
go into it, do we?
Henery No . . .
Miss Mullett No . . .

*Miss Mullett goes out into the garden and goes off in the direction Aubrey
and company have taken*

*Henery, still at the double doors, watches her go and then peeks out into the
hall*

Henery (*calling softly*) Sprules! Sprules!

*He goes off into the hall, calling and making the "nose" sign clicking noise.
Before he has gone very far he turns, remembering to shut the double doors
behind him*

*Maitland comes in from the garden, almost at once. He still looks extremely
puzzled. He stares round the room and after a second crosses to the double
doors. He pauses, his hand on one of the door handles. He opens the door*

*Henery enters simultaneously, opening both doors. He keeps hold of the
other end of the door handle Maitland is grasping*

Both men stand either side of the door unable to see each other. Maitland looks back towards the french windows. Henery closes the other double door (i.e. the one Maitland isn't behind). Maitland looks suspicious. Henery now makes to close the other door, placing his hand over Maitland's in order to do so. They close the door together. Both slowly look down to discover they are in effect holding hands. Their eyes slowly meet. They both react and then glare at each other

Maitland What the——? Who the——? How the——? Where the——?

Maitland, menacingly, takes off his hat and places it carefully on a table. Henery takes off his own hat and hands it to Maitland who is about to do the same again when he realizes what he is doing and hurls Henery's hat angrily on the floor. Maitland pounces on Henery and seizes him by the throat. He forces Henery to the ground. Both are invisible behind the settle. We see moments of a furious fight. Finally, Henery shakily regains his feet. Maitland lunges at him, Henery side-steps and Maitland crashes into the fireplace bringing half the chimney stack down around him. Henery flees into the garden one way, nearly runs into . . .

Giles entering with his pitchfork

Henery turns about and runs back through the house and out by way of the double doors. As he reaches these . . .

Sprules enters from the hall to investigate the commotion

Henery nearly runs into him. He gives Sprules a feverish "nose" sign and rushes past him into the hall as he hears Giles in pursuit

Sprules (*ecstatically*) Henery!

Sprules exits after Henery into the hall

Giles comes in from the garden with his pitchfork in pursuit of Henery. Maitland is just regaining his feet, having dragged himself out of the fireplace. Giles charges at Maitland with the fork, thinking he is Henery. Maitland seizes the fork by the prongs and bends them angrily

Maitland (*as he does this*) Not me, you fool! The other one! After him! (*He points towards the hall*)

Giles, alarmed, runs off through the hall

(*Staggering*) It's a madhouse or a bunch of crooks! (*Yelling*) Jean! Jean!

Jean comes rushing on from the garden followed first by Aubrey and Louise and then Chesterman and Miss Mullett

Jean (*alarmed*) What is it, darling? Are you all right, George?
Maitland Who's the man who's just gone out?
Jean Man, darling?
Maitland Like me, he's gone through that door. He looked exactly like me.
Jean (*soothingly*) Yes, darling, yes.
Maitland You'd better believe me, there was this man——

Louise What man?

At this moment Henery, pursued by Giles, comes rushing through from the hall, on his way to the garden

Maitland That man. He's an impostor after him!

Sprules rushes through in pursuit of Henery. He sees Maitland

Sprules Henery! (*He embraces Maitland*)
Maitland (*pushing him away*) Not me, you fool, the other one.

Sprules goes out after Henery

(*Dragging Jean with him*) After him!

Maitland takes off in pursuit through the french windows

Jean (*excitedly as she goes*) He's an impostor. After him.

She follows Maitland off

Miss Mullett and Chesterman, both rather startled by all this activity, follow them off

Miss Mullett
Chesterman } (*together*) After him!

Miss Mullett and Chesterman exit

Louise and Aubrey regard each other helplessly

Aubrey Louise, there are two of them!
Louise Yes.
Aubrey But which one's the real one?
Louise I haven't the faintest idea, Aubrey. They're probably breeding.
Aubrey Oh, love a duck!

Henery, followed by Giles, followed by Maitland and Jean, followed by Miss Mullett and Chesterman, chase across the garden behind them

Neither appears to notice

Louise Aubrey—I've got an idea.
Aubrey I'll never die again as long as I live.
Louise No, darling, you shan't. This time you shall come to life.
Aubrey What's the good of that?
Louise What's the good of it? Listen. Clear out and put on an old suit of clothes—make yourself as dirty and untidy as possible.
Aubrey Yes?
Louise Wait till they're all in here and then stagger in through the garden— in a dazed condition.
Aubrey Yes.
Louise Act!! You've lost your memory. The shock of the explosion. You weren't killed. You've been wandering about ever since.
Aubrey By Jove!

Louise You've come back here—you see me—the old home—it all comes back to you—they don't contradict you and—(*triumphantly*)—the money's ours!

Henery, followed by Giles, chases back across the garden

Aubrey Right! I'll do it! I'm glad I thought of that.

Voices are heard off

Louise Quick! I hear them.

Aubrey bolts out through the double doors

Louise places Aubrey's monk's staff in the fireplace

At that moment, Maitland, Jean, Chesterman and Miss Mullett come in through the windows, excitedly

Maitland He's got clean away!

Chesterman I suppose you are really George Maitland?

Maitland Say, has this house gone plumb crazy?

Louise Certainly not, Cousin George, but——

Maitland Well, if this house is the English idea of hospitality to a man who's come three thousand miles, it's me for Mexico every time.

Jean But, George dear——

Maitland You keep out of the way, Little Blossom. I'm not blaming you. Now, Mr Lawyer, let's hear from you.

Chesterman It's simply, Mr Maitland, we've had two impostors here in the last two days. But no doubt you've got papers in your pocket to prove your identity?

Maitland Papers! I'm as full of papers as a bookstall. And if I could have got someone to talk horse sense when I first arrived you'd have got 'em long ago.

Miss Mullett (*alarmed to see the monk's staff in the fireplace*) Louise, where's that monk?

Louise Er—I don't know.

Chesterman Oh, doubtless he'll turn up again in a minute.

Louise Yes, I shouldn't be a bit surprised if he does.

Miss Mullett I wanted to question him more closely about his knots.

Maitland (*giving papers to Chesterman*) Just take a look over those, Mr Lawyer. If anyone wants to dispute my identity, come on, let's start disputing. (*He looks menacing*)

Chesterman (*hastily examining the papers*) Well, it's something to know we've found the rightful heir at last, Mr Maitland. It looks as if all our troubles are over now.

Jean No. This is really George Maitland.

Miss Mullett We're sure to find he isn't, of course.

Jean George—you can kiss me.

They kiss. Miss Mullett starts on her knitting. Chesterman reads Maitland's papers

Miss Mullett That's the third man she's kissed in two days.
Jean (*surfacing*) I could have told you anywhere, George, by the way you kiss!

From the garden, the sound of someone strumming a discordant banjo. Everyone looks up, startled

Aubrey appears outside the windows. He wanders past without apparently noticing the occupants of the room. He looks very dazed; he is dirty, and wears oddly matched clothes. A light coat, dark trousers, an old straw hat and white canvas shoes; he carries a banjo

Aubrey (*as he passes the window*) Banjo!
Louise (*with a shriek*) Aubrey—my husband!

The all react

Alive! Alive! You're not a ghost?
Aubrey (*dazed*) Who are you?
Louise I'm Louise—Aubrey—your own little wife.
Aubrey Where am I?
Louise In your home, darling—your old home.
Aubrey My old home! The same old home—the same little wife!
Louise (*indicating Miss Mullett*) And you know who this is?

Aubrey, very moved, goes to Miss Mullett and drops in front of her on one knee

Aubrey Mammy!
Louise No, dear, it's Auntie ...
Aubrey The same old Auntie! The same old knitting!
Louise And there's Mr Chesterman, the lawyer——
Aubrey The same old liar!
Louise —who came to tell us about the money.
Aubrey Money? Money? I've heard of that somewhere.

During the next, Sprules and Simpson appear in the hall and move to listen, unobtrusively, just inside the double doors

Similarly Giles, returning from the chase, stops outside the french windows for the next

Henery appears at yet another window

Louise Aubrey, can't you remember? The blasting powder! The explosion!
Aubrey Explosion! Explosion! Oh, it all comes back to me!
All Yes, yes!
Aubrey Like—like a returned cheque.
All Yes, yes!
Aubrey I was alone—by myself—in the shed.
Jean Yes, yes!
Aubrey I was working.
All Yes, yes!

Aubrey I don't know why.

All No, no!

Aubrey Suddenly there was a crash!

All Yes, yes!

Aubrey A sheem of flate ...

Louise (*trying to help him*) A shame of fleet.

Aubrey A street of shame.

All Yes, yes!

Aubrey And—and—and everything seemed to go up, up, up, then it came down, down, down, and round and round and round, and here we are again!

Aubrey and Louise embrace. Everyone applauds

Sprules, Simpson, Giles and Henery withdraw quietly

Miss Mullett continues to knit. Maitland and Jean embrace. A slight pause. The phone rings

Chesterman (*tentatively*) I'll answer the phone, Mr Allington. (*He takes the receiver and holds a silent conversation*)

Maitland Yes, but where do I come in?

Aubrey You don't!

Louise Aubrey dear, this is Cousin George from Mexico.

Aubrey So you're the fellow who gets the money when I'm dead.

Maitland (*angrily*) But you are dead.

Aubrey Oh no, I'm not!

Maitland Well, there's something crooked about the whole business I want explained. Here am I fetched all the way from Vera Cruz ...

Aubrey Don't mention that woman's name! I'm alive and the money's mine.

Maitland The money's mine, you're dead.

Aubrey You can dispute it until you're blue in the face.

Maitland The money's mine, and I'm going to have it.

Aubrey If you can get it, you're welcome to it.

Chesterman (*replacing the receiver, loudly*) One moment, please, one moment! Gentlemen! I've just received a message from my office. Your brother's estate has just been cleared up and I am now in a position to issue——

Aubrey Bless you!

Chesterman —a cheque for the whole amount.

Maitland You pay that money to me.

Aubrey You'll do nothing of the kind; you'll pay that money to me.

Chesterman One moment, please. After deducting expenses, death duties and the usual fees, the estate has realized eighty-seven thousand, six hundred pounds.

Maitland You pay that to me.

Jean To him.

Aubrey No, to me.

Louise To us.

Chesterman Ladies and gentlemen, please. Allow me to finish. I say eighty-seven thousand six hundred less a confiscation of certain money by the Alaskan—(*he gives Aubrey a wary glance*)—government, leaving the sum total of one pound four shillings and fourpence halfpenny. (*He laughs*)

All parties look despairing, especially Aubrey and Louise

Sprules enters through the double doors

Sprules The butcher, the baker, the dairymaid, the florist, the tailor, the milliner, the wine merchant, the laundrywoman and the coalman, sir.
Aubrey Oh, wheel them all in, Sprules.
Sprules (*mildly shocked*) Into the drawing room, sir?
Aubrey Why not? It belongs to them now, anyway. You'd better lay dinner for twenty-five as well, Sprules.
Sprules Very good, sir.

Sprules withdraws

A pause

Louise Aubrey!
Aubrey Yes, darling?
Louise I've got an idea!

Aubrey backs away from her shaking his head. Louise, still trying to sell him her new "idea", pursues him. Maitland and Jean move in demanding their share, Chesterman follows, waving the cheque he has just written. Aubrey starts to climb up the wall in a vain attempt to escape, first on to the mantelshelf and then higher still

As he does this the doors open again and Sprules attempts over the ensuing hub-bub to announce the crowd of tradespeople who enter waving bills and angrily demanding payment

Miss Mullett, oblivious, continues her knitting. On this hectic scene —

the Curtain *falls*

FURNITURE AND PROPERTY LIST

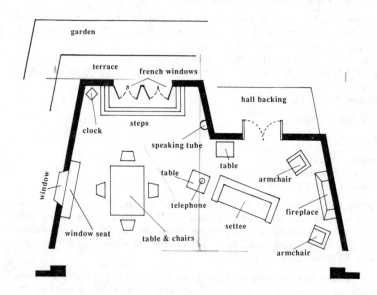

ACT I

On stage: Armchairs
Bronze statuette with electrolier
Settle couch. *On it:* cushions
Small table. *On it:* telephone
Bookcase with books
Low cabinet. *In wall above it:* speaking tube
Grandfather clock
Fireplace. *In hearth:* irons. *Near it:* bell-pull
Fender stool
Sideboard. *In it:* photograph album
Gate-legged table. *On it:* tablecloth, breakfast settings
2 upright chairs
On walls: tapestries, coat of arms over fireplace
Carpet

Off stage: Silver salver with letters, bills, writs, morning paper **(Sprules)**
Tray with hot dishes, coffee, milk **(Simpson)**
Hat with 3 eggs **(Giles)**
Attaché case containing will **(Chesterman)**

Flowers **(Giles)**
Tray **(Simpson)**
Knitting **(Miss Mullett)**
Telegram **(Simpson)**
Cucumber **(Giles)**
Charred, smouldering tablecloth **(Sprules)**
Debris from explosion **(Stage Management)**

Personal: **Aubrey:** monocle, pocket watch
Miss Mullet: wrist watch

ACT II

Strike: Eggs, cucumber, flowers, charred tablecloth, debris from explosion, letters, telegram, photograph album, **Miss Mullett**'s knitting

Set: Novel for **Louise**

Off stage: Butler's table/tray with tea things for 4, tea-cloth **(Simpson)**
Wheelbarrow **(Giles)**
Knitting needle **(Miss Mullett)**
Teapot **(Simpson)**
Glass of water **(Chesterman)**
Basket of gooseberries **(Giles)**
Tray **(Simpson)**
3 or 4 trays **(Sprules)**
Bread **(Simpson)**
Chair **(Giles)**
Knitting bag with knitting **(Sprules)**
Bundle of clothes **(Louise)**
Bundle of clothes **(Sprules)**
Bundle of clothes **(Giles)**
Boat cushions, duckweed **(Aubrey)**

Personal: **Louise:** handkerchief
Jean: handbag with mirror, make-up

ACT III

Strike: Glass, basket of gooseberries, bundle of clothes, novel

Set: Double doors open
Miss Mullett's knitting under cushion on settle

Off stage: Hat **(Henery)**
Attaché case containing 2 telegrams, chequebook, pen **(Chesterman)**
Pitchfork **(Giles)**
Knitting **(Miss Mullet)**
Banjo **(Aubrey)**
Bills **(Tradespeople)**

Personal: **Sprules:** handkerchief
Aubrey: staff
Maitland: papers

LIGHTING PLOT

Property fittings required: electrolier, chandelier

Interior and exterior. A library and terrace

ACT I.   Morning

To open: General lighting

No cues

ACT II.   Afternoon

To open: General lighting

No cues

ACT III.   Late afternoon

To open: General lighting

No cues

EFFECTS PLOT

ACT I

Cue 1	As CURTAIN rises *Telephone rings; after slight pause, it rings again*	(Page 1)
Cue 2	**Louise:** "What!!!" (*She gazes at Giles in horror*) *Tremendous explosion*	(Page 17)
Cue 3	All rush out through the double doors *Smoke outside french windows*	(Page 17)

ACT II

Cue 4	Shortly after CURTAIN rises *Telephone rings*	(Page 19)
Cue 5	**Chesterman:** "They're just like lovers." *Floor creaks upstairs, chandelier swings a couple of times*	(Page 28)

ACT III

Cue 6	**Simpson** tries to soothe **Sprules** *Doorbell*	(Page 40)
Cue 7	**Simpson:** "Mr Sprules——!" *Doorbell*	(Page 40)
Cue 8	**Maitland** and **Jean** embrace. A slight pause *Telephone rings*	(Page 58)

MADE AND PRINTED IN GREAT BRITAIN BY
LATIMER TREND & COMPANY LTD PLYMOUTH

MADE IN ENGLAND